THE NEW MODERNS

THE NEW MODERNS

JONATHAN GLANCEY AND RICHARD BRYANT

MITCHELL BEAZLEY

THE NEW MODERNS
Text by Jonathan Glancey
Photography by Richard Bryant

First published in Great Britain in 1990
by Mitchell Beazley
an imprint of Reed Books Limited,
Michelin House, 81 Fulham Road,
London SW3 6RB
and Auckland and Melbourne

First published in paperback in 1994
Reprinted 1995, 1996, 1997

Senior Executive Art Editor **Jacqui Small**
Executive Editor **Judith More**
Art Editor **Christopher Howson**
Editorial Assistant **Jaspal Kharay**
Production **Ted Timberlake, Sarah Schuman**

ISBN 1 85732 438 2

A CIP record for this book is available from the British Library

Set in Trade Gothic Roman 9/11pt and 8/10pt
Colour reproduction by Scantrans Pte Ltd, Singapore
Produced by Mandarin Book Production

Printed and bound in Hong Kong

"Architecture is the masterly,
correct and magnificent play of
masses brought together in light."

LE CORBUSIER
Vers une Architecture

C·O·N·T·E·N·T·S

Foreword

Modernism, as we have known it, has served as the aesthetic, spiritual and moral conscience of our time. It embodies the essentially democratic idea of the creative artist as the inventor of a personal style, a unique vision of the world. Modernism fosters a dynamic intellectual climate, based upon the obligation to question, analyze and criticize in the exhaustive search for truth.

Modernism has also served a subversive function by articulating ideas and sense perceptions at odds with the prevailing aesthetic or sociocultural order. It has challenged the dominance of that order, thus provoking reevaluation, overturning preconceptions and offering new perspectives and values. Picasso and Braque are an example of two artists who, in their relentless and competitive investigation of perceptual alternatives, forever changed our way of seeing.

Modernism has also established criticism as an integral discipline in the process. In its worst form of protectionism, criticism can become a kind of court, where the critics are the judges and the architects/artists are the defendants who are frequently found guilty and sentenced to failure for daring to question the status quo. I believe critics have the responsibility to counter bureaucratic and academic taboos; to advance the cause of an architecture that reflects economic, technological and sociocultural factors. Criticism should champion a better quality of life and the creative expression of the individual and collective imagination, rather than an unquestioned historicism.

Architects create art, not by reestablishing the established, but by destabilizing the status quo. Modern architecture forces us to believe that this process is more important and always more satisfying than the comfort of the known.

At last! *The New Moderns* is a book of clarity, conviction, and historical importance. Richard Bryant's photographs are full of poetry and insight without being falsely romantic. Jonathan Glancey's text is spirited and pertinently biased, extraordinarily readable and convincing, because it is both passionate and accurate. Together, they have produced a testament to modern architecture and use of space that is both inspiring and essential.

CHARLES GWATHMEY

OPEL HOUSE
VERMONT, USA
CHARLES GWATHMEY

Introduction

Today, people throughout the developed world can choose to build and furnish their homes in any style, historic or modern. Europe and America are littered with pseudo-historic and Post-Modern buildings. However, it is intriguing to see that some wealthy people are tiring of the visual clutter and sheer bulk of too many worldly possessions and discarding these in favor of more austere homes. The work of minimalist architects as John Pawson and Claudio Silvestrin proves that there is a demand for houses as simple and chaste as a traditional Japanese dwelling or a 13th century Cistercian monastery. It is also the case that as property prices continue to rise, despite cyclical fluctuations, in the world's major cities people are forced to look for smaller and smaller homes. In this situation it is far better to make the optimum use of space, rather than diminishing it by the accumulation of too many possessions.

The New Moderns are those people who have begun and will increasingly choose a clean, spacious, light and clutter-free architecture in the 1990s and beyond. They are pioneers in the true sense because they have the vision and strength to jump clear over the hurdle of fake historic styles and look to a contemporary way of living that makes sense in today's noisy, intense, consumerist world.

THE STORER HOUSE, CALIFORNIA, USA FRANK LLOYD WRIGHT

1, 2 & 3. Designed in 1923, this house was a radical departure from traditional North American houses. However, with its combination of flat roofs, open-plan interiors, local materials and stylized ethnic details and decoration it made the Modern house both a thoroughly new experience and as natural as any of its predecessors.

1

2

3

4. Living rooms inside the Storer House were designed to make optimum use of daylight. The intention was to create a sense of warmth and well-being through the forms of the architecture and the richness of the materials, together with a play of light through and across them. Many of Wright's techniques in house design have been taken up by later architects, designers and decorators.

4

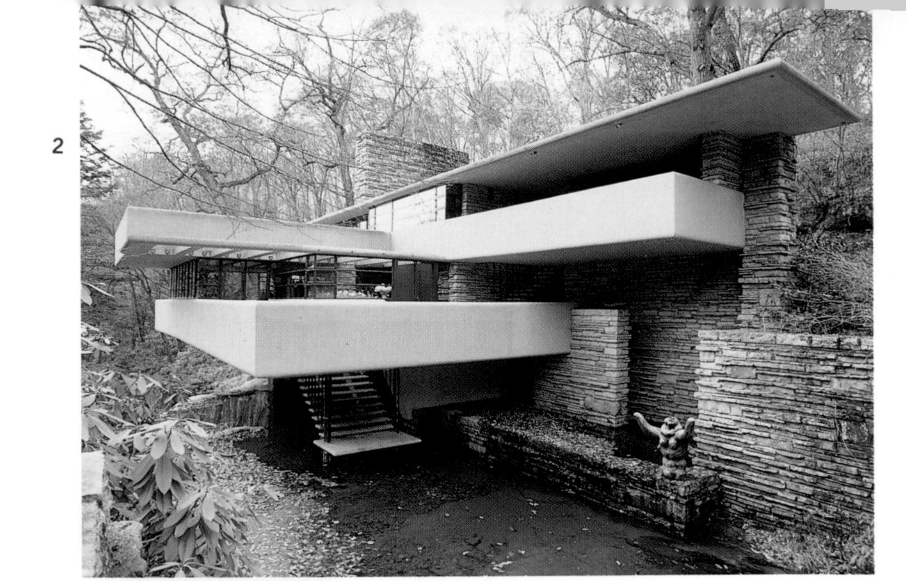

But if uninspired architects have harmed the reputation of Modern architecture, mass production has damaged its reputation even further. After the Second World War, millions of new houses had to be built across Europe and Japan. New mass production techniques and materials enabled governments to build rapidly using prefabricated systems. But these techniques were all too often untried and insufficiently tested. The result was a spate of rashly considered, poorly detailed and patchily built housing that a global public associated with Modern architecture. In the public mind, crass prefabricated public housing was bagged together with the stunning new houses designed by architects of real genius – Frank Lloyd Wright and Le Corbusier among them.

If just a small percentage of Europeans had seen representative examples of high-quality Modern architecture in the 1950s and 1960s, the nostalgia boom might never have grown as it did. Despite problems of public recognition and understanding, throughout the world, as this book reveals, excellent Modern houses have been built.

The remarkable thing about New Modern houses is their variety. To many people, the word Modern conjures up a vision of some nightmare concrete jungle. But concrete is not a prerequisite

ROBIE HOUSE
CHICAGO, USA,
FRANK LLOYD WRIGHT

Previous page: In this house of 1907–9, Wright based his design on long, flowing horizontal lines. The house, a mix of traditional materials and details and a composition of abstract planes and volumes, still has the power to shock.

They are visionaries because they have seen that what has passed for Modern architecture over the past 40 years has, on the whole, been unworthy of the name. Modern buildings are difficult to design well. Because Modernism offered architects, designers and their clients almost complete freedom to build and decorate in innovative ways, many made mistakes. Traditional rules of architecture, especially those of Classicism, prevent second-rate architects and builders from making too many gross errors of proportion, taste and decorative detail. However, Modernism offers far too much freedom and discretion to architects and designers, many of whom have clearly need a framework of rules in which to work. When architects followed rules and codes laid down by the grammarians of the Classical language of architecture, they satisfied their public. But when Modernism suggested to each and every one of them that they might be individual geniuses, each one a Le Corbusier or Frank Lloyd Wright, many failed to meet the challenge.

FALLINGWATER
PENNSYLVANIA, USA
FRANK LLOYD WRIGHT

1. This long sweep of living space is based partly on the seamless flow of the decks of an ocean liner, partly on traditional Japanese design. New Modern architects are influenced by the same sources.
2. This house of 1935–9 is a play of geometric architectural planes set on rocks and over a waterfall.
3. Fallingwater is proof that a Modern house can work with and even enhance nature. Here, concrete terraces jut out over the waterfall.

4

5

6

for a Modern house. A Modern architect can choose to build in traditional wood; stone or brick; or select contemporary options like steel, aluminum, plastics and polymers. Modernism does not mean the end of fine craftsmanship. In fact, quite the reverse is true. When a house is designed to be simple and sparing in its use of decoration, each detail assumes an importance. Modern architecture requires great precision if it is to be convincing. The much-celebrated German architect Mies van der Rohe, a purist among Moderns, once said "God is in the details." Once seen, a Modern house begins to win adherents.

But what are the qualities in a house that the New Moderns look for? What distinguishes a New Modern home from pseudo-historic and Post-Modern alternatives? The following pages seek to analyze, one by one, the key features of New Modern design. These qualities, which are gradually winning more and more people over to a New Modern esthetic, are space, light, versatility and freedom from clutter. Modern space flows. Conventional

THE VILLA SAVOIE
POISSY, FRANCE
LE CORBUSIER

4. Built 1929–31, this is the most influential of the early, pure white, Modern houses.

5 & 6. Le Corbusier chose to describe the Modern house as a "machine for living in." His machines fit for the human pysche were full of elegant, flowing spaces such as the stairwell in the Villa Savoie (left) or else designed for hygiene and relaxation together (above).

2

rooms disappear, to be replaced by a seamless sequence of living spaces which produce light and airy interiors that make optimum use of available space. Without conventional walls separating rooms, daylight flows through a New Modern interior. Mezzanine levels and open stairs dispense with conventional gloomy corridors.

The New Modern house offers a chance to start from first principles. How do you really want your living accommodation arranged? Free from conventional planning, a Modern house can be a single large living space or else a complex sequence of interlocking living spaces. In the hands of an architect like David Wild, a New Modern house can offer generous living spaces in the tightest of city plots. Wild's twin London houses have very different interiors, providing accommodation for people with radically different lifestyles. A conventional housebuilder would have provided two identical interiors and expected householders to adapt to the constrictions that conventional house plans impose. But David Wild has been able to offer the purchasers of his houses flexibility. To step into a double-height living room in a fairly modest city home is a remarkable experience. New Modern living is generous, even when space is at a premium.

Out in the country, the New Modern house comes into its own. Surrounding gardens and countryside are seen to their best advantage from houses in which internal barriers are few and far between. Some Modern architects have chosen to design houses in the countryside that, pure and white, act as a foil to surrounding nature, much like Greek temples. Others have chosen to build in local materials, allowing their houses to be gently absorbed by their surroundings. New Modern style is flexible, adaptable and appropriate to both urban and rural ways of life.

New Modern houses do make some special demands on their owners and occupiers. Often more clean-cut than conventional counterparts,

3

1, 2, 3 & 4. Certain design themes and materials run right through the history of the Modern and the New Modern house. One of these is the use of glass bricks. In fact, glass brick has become an icon as well as a commonly integral part of the structure of many 20th century houses. Glass bricks, like their baked clay counterparts, are capable of carrying weight, but they also allow light to diffuse gently through rooms and spaces. The play of light in a New Modern house is an essential part of its character, and the glass brick has long added to the possibilities of manipulating light, both natural and artificial.

4

3

1

2

they rarely suit clutter. Most families are surrounded by possessions, so a New Modern architect will provide ample built-in storage. Beyond this, it is generally true that each piece of furniture, each painting, each object takes on a greater presence than it would in a traditional home. This encourages people to look anew at their possessions. The badly designed and the poorly made suddenly seem out of place. New Modern living offers a chance to rethink a lifestyle that has become bogged down in domestic detritus.

The New Moderns are not a uniform group. Around the world, Modern housing adopts any number of forms and imbues any number of local, regional and national characteristics. A New Modern house might grow organically from an old building, or it might be a celebration of new ideas in esthetics and materials. It might be in the heart of the city or set deep in the countryside. But what the New Modern house offers above all is an escape from bogus history, from the mean constraints of conventional house plans, and from pseudo-country taste. This freedom is demanding because it requires the exercise of personal taste, rather than the mimicking of given style. Because of this, the New Modern way of building and living is unlikely to supplant the traditional, but it does offer a viable and very attractive alternative.

1, 2 & 3. New Modern houses are composed of abstract planes and volumes. Simple in Modern houses of the 1920s and 1930s, now these are often rich and complex. The New Modern house is both a high-minded game of abstract art and an inviting home. Such a New Modern house can be enjoyed on both an intellectual and sensual level.

1

2

The mastery of space

ROGERS' HOUSE
LONDON, ENGLAND
RICHARD ROGERS

1. The open and dynamic interrelationship between interior spaces is a theme at the heart of the New Modern house. Conventional, box-like rooms give way to a seamless flow of light, airy and friendly space.
2. Space is one of the most precious commodities in cities and yet in virtually all houses it is meanly sacrificed in favour of a conventional room layout, even when this leads to tiny, dark or ill-proportioned rooms. This double-height living room is the antithesis of this endemic meanness: pure, unadulterated space.

Modernism began as a reaction against excessive decoration and more specifically the rich, swaggering imperial baroque architecture of the years between the turn of the 20th century and the First World War. However, the early Moderns' most important contribution to the design of the house was their attempt to turn accepted ideas of the nature of a house inside out. To them, what mattered was the plan. A house should be designed from the inside out. While this led to some distinguished Modern villas in the 1920s and 1930s, these were essentially selfish one-offs. Set in the countryside or on the fringes of suburbs they were fine, but in the heart of historic cities Modern houses and apartment blocks played an increasingly destructive role. The New Moderns take issue with the selfish impact of early Modern houses. They believe that in towns and cities new housing must be a good neighbor to historical precedent and that there is a balance to be struck between interior and facade.

The impact of the first truly Modern houses must have been astonishing. The free-flowing spaces of the interiors of Le Corbusier's villas, such as the Villa Savoie, Poissy, France (see page 15), of Richard Neutra's Lovell House in California (1927–9), of Pierre Chareau's *Maison de Verre* in Paris, France (1928–32) and Gerrit Rietveld's Schroder house in Utrecht, Holland (1924) were truly revolutionary. One of the central ideas in all these houses was that the interior plan was the

1. Almost everything that could be done has been done to create the maximum possible free space from this large room. Even the radiators have been reduced to a minimal size, while the neutral finishes make the most of precious London sunlight.

2. The freestanding kitchen unit makes cooking an easy and sociable occasion, while the ceiling-height cabinets, fronted in stainless steel, ensure that domestic detritus can be stowed away in ship-shape fashion. This is, after all, a living space.

generator of the architecture. The appearance of the building was determined by the arrangement of internal space.

This can be seen clearly in these early Modern houses as their living rooms become balconies that jut out into the open. As Theo Van Doesburg's De Stijl manifesto, *16 Points of a Plastic Architecture,* pointed out in 1923, the new architecture was ". . . . anti-cubic. That is to say, it does not try to freeze the different functional space cells in one enclosed cube. Rather it throws the functional space cells, as well as the overhanging planes (balcony volumes), centrifugally from the core of the cube. And through the means of height, width and depth – plus time, an imaginary four-dimensional entity – the new architecture approaches a totally new plastic expression in open spaces. In this way architecture acquires a more or less floating aspect that, so to speak, works against the gravitational forces of nature."

3. The Rogers' house is a transformation of an early 19th century, stucco-fronted London house. Its regular proportions and large windows made it an ideal starting point for a New Modern interior. The eight lit windows on the upper floors illuminate just one room. (For an inside view see pp. 20–21).

4. This blue steel pillar creates a powerful divide between the clean-cut, solid forms of the kitchen and the complex and spidery roof and stairscape. The architect has used materials – stainless steel, rolled steel, wood and glass – that create their own visual and tactile tension.

Although wrapped in a contemporary pseudo-scientific jargon, it is easy enough to understand what Van Doesburg was driving at. After years of heavy-handed architecture, the Modern iconoclasts wanted to create light and airy buildings that floated free from prevailing taste. The best interiors of the 1920s and 1930s remain refreshing. They coincided with a revolution in domestic social life. Although many early Modern houses still incorporated extensive accommodation for domestic staff, the family itself was a less rigid social unit. The open-plan nature of Modern interiors encouraged people to mix rather than to hide away in their rooms. Children were to be seen and heard. Sunshine was encouraged to flow through the various interconnecting spaces and rooms.

The free-flowing space, double-height rooms with galleries and mezzanines, open-plan stairs and top lights that admit sunlight to potentially gloomy interior spaces established by the early Moderns are even more attractive characteristics today, when property prices in many of the world's cities are so enormously high. Now, more than ever, space is a luxury in the city. And the New Modern approach provides ways of optimizing that space, as the houses and interiors shown in this book prove. In houses where space is not at a premium, a New Modern interior and its occupants revel in the sheer freedom of space obtainable and

WYCHCOMBE STUDIOS
LONDON, ENGLAND
RICK MATHER ARCHITECTS

1. The route through a New Modern interior is a journey through inner space. The relationship between different parts of these interiors is a dynamic one: exciting oppositions, as here, can be set up between old and new elements.

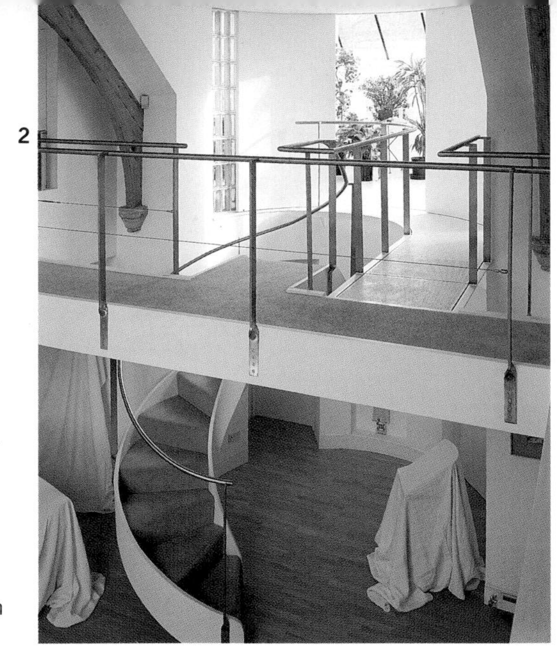

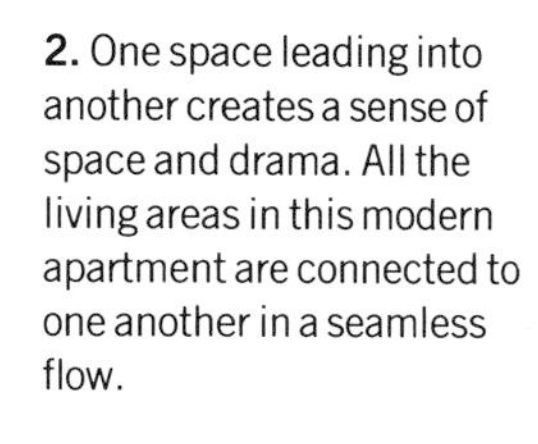

2. One space leading into another creates a sense of space and drama. All the living areas in this modern apartment are connected to one another in a seamless flow.

3. The main living space is kept dramatically simple and uncluttered, creating an effect like a stage set where people can act out their everyday lives. High ceilings add high drama to compact apartments.

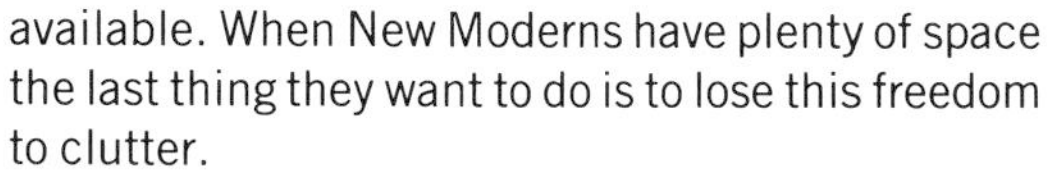

available. When New Moderns have plenty of space the last thing they want to do is to lose this freedom to clutter.

A New Modern interior can be spoiled with too much furniture or too many objects. The secret of success is to pare down to a minimum. Let the space do the work, revel in the generous expanses a New Modern interior offers and indulge in a few objects that might never even fit into a conventional interior. It is the space itself that is so attractive, so it is always a shame to eat into that space unnecessarily. This is certainly the view taken by architects such as John Pawson and Claudio Silvestrin, who have designed some of the most minimal of all modern houses and apartments.

But space of this sort is demanding in other ways. It shows the dirt and it shows up flaws in construction. Wallpaper is an easy way of hiding badly plastered walls. Glued-on reproduction moldings can disguise unsatisfactory meetings between wall and ceiling. Fitted carpets can cover up floors in poor condition. Devoid of such disguises, the New Modern interior needs to be solidly built and well-finished. Modern housing first acquired its bad

4. The stair in a New Modern house can be just as much a domestic sculpture as a mundane way of moving between lower and higher levels. This stainless steel and chrome creation is a modern way of looking at an ancient device—the spiral stair.

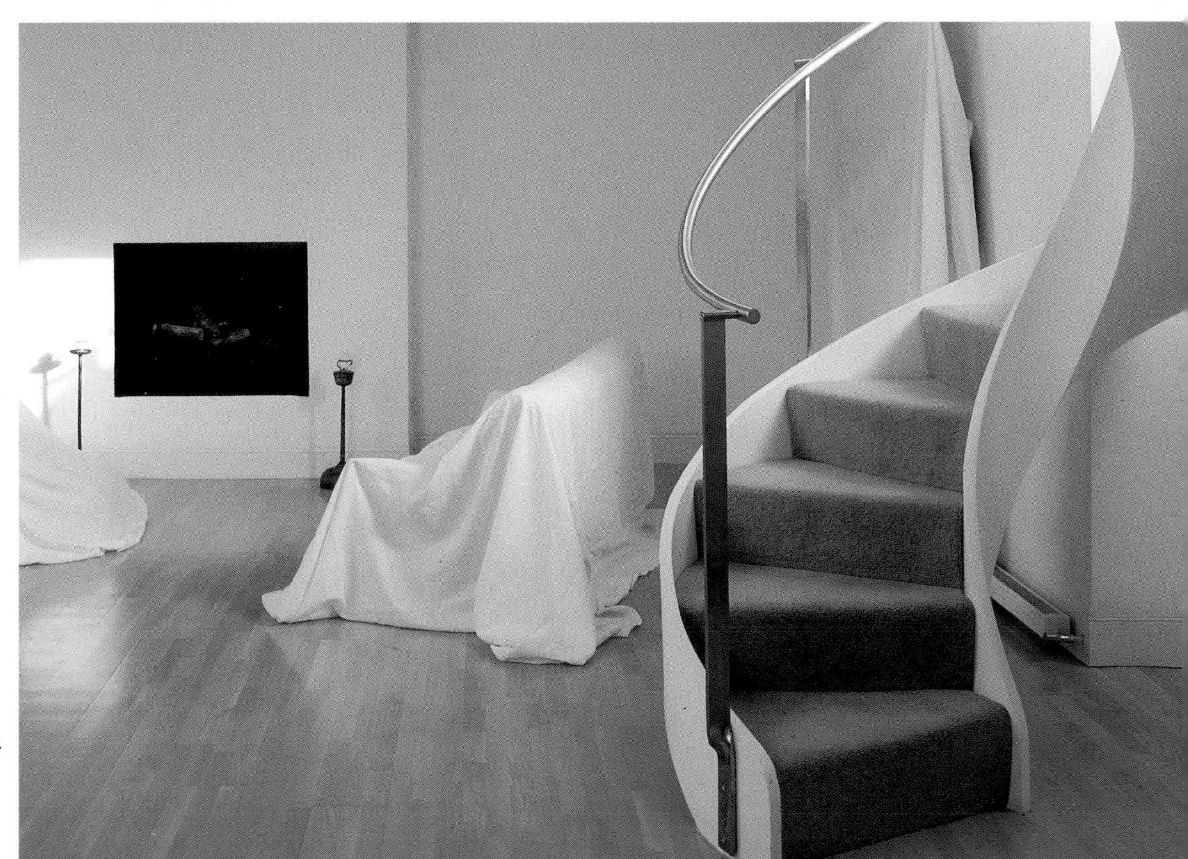

POWER STATION HOUSE
TEXAS, USA
GARY CUNNINGHAM

1. Projecting out from this palazzo of power is a balcony that draws its inspiration from the surrounding industrial imagery: in this case from the pylon behind.
2. Internal drama is achieved by the ways in which walls and partitions are layered. This creates a richness that might only otherwise be achieved through decorative treatment.
3. By not pretending that this is anything other than an old industrial building, the interior is rich in powerful imagery: grim chains are now lively decoration.
4. This room could be described as the apotheosis of Modernism. Modern Movement architects and designers have long drawn on industry and technology for their imagery. Here, that imagery is reconciled with warm wood surfaces and a sense of luxury conveyed by uninterrupted space.

reputation in the 1960s and 1970s simply because so much of it the world over was so badly built. Many older houses were also damp, drafty, out-of-alignment and generally ailing, but these flaws could always be disguised. It was also the case that many so-called modern houses and apartment blocks were not really Modern at all. They were simply badly arranged conventional buildings with ugly, stripped-back exteriors: discomfort without the charm of old buildings.

The influences at work on the handling of space in New Modern interiors are as complex as the interiors themselves appear simple. Undoubtedly, one of the most significant influences has been that of the traditional Japanese interior, which offered a flexible use of space and subtle changes in light. Moveable screens provided privacy when necessary, while daylight filtered through their translucent paper coverings. The net effect of this was to create oases of domestic sanity in even the most crowded city. Lasting influences also include those

1. In a converted building like this old power station, which was never designed to be lived in, space and light have to be manipulated in dramatic ways. In this view of the dining area, the architect's handling of space enables shafts of sunlight to shoot across the floor, then ricochet off the blonde wood door.

2. Large industrial spaces can be very easy to live in if divided in subtle New Modern ways. Space can be modulated using varied textures for wall surfaces and partitions. Here, a screen of milky glass contrasts with a deliberately industrial breeze-block partition, the warm red original brickwork of the external walls and the shining ductwork.

of the early Modern Movement architects, in particular Le Corbusier, Eileen Gray, Richard Neutra and Frank Lloyd Wright. Wright, in turn, was much influenced by traditional Japanese interiors. A further influence on New Modern architecture has been the *Maison de Verre*, Pierre Chareau's astonishing house in Paris, France. Built in the 1920s, it was the first house to domesticate the industrial esthetic. Chareau has been a considerable influence on the work of contemporary architects such as Richard Rogers and Eva Jiricna. But perhaps the most important influence of all has been the desire of New Moderns to escape from the spatial strictures of traditional and developer's houses.

CUBIST APARTMENT
NEW YORK, USA
STEVEN HOLL

1. One of the great influences on New Modern thinking is Russian Constructivism, in which walls often adopted odd and pronounced angles. Steven Holl has used this approach to dramatic, if chaste, effect in this apartment in which the interpretation of space is the driving force.
2. The apartment is composed of a sequence of interlocking spaces. This demanding esthetic has been carried rigorously through each room, down to the design of cupboards and lockers. Undecorated textures and minimal use of furniture maximize space.

1

NICK KNIGHT HOUSE
SURREY, ENGLAND
DAVID CHIPPERFIELD

1 & 2. The formal garden, defined by the external concrete frame, is a stop-gap between the house and the conventional garden that extends beyond. The purpose is to create a transitional zone between the formal qualities of the man-made house and the equally formal, yet softer forms of the natural world. This also acts as an outside room, in the manner of a Japanese garden (see p.171).

3. The living room of this house is designed to appear to extend into a further room beyond the sheer glass walls. When the trees mature, the effect will be one of contrast between the hard edges of the man-made space and the soft, green texture of the natural space beyond.

2

4. The meeting between two sheer plates of glass is the minimal divide between the living room and the garden "room," beyond. Outside, the pool refracts sparkling light into both spaces.

3

1

2

1. In the hallway a change of floor surface from wood to polished granite marks the transition from the inside world to the street outside. This shift in texture is both practical and serves to demarcate different spaces with disparate uses.

2. The walls of this sequence of interior spaces need no decoration; decorative treatments could only reduce the beautiful effects created by daylight playing on walls and floors from a number of hidden and revealed sources. Pools of light add to the richness of already generous space.

1

1. Cooking is not a solitary activity in this house: standing behind the hob, the view extends directly into the dining area, over the table and out into the sheltered garden beyond. The kitchen looks both ways – out over the sinks into the street in one direction, and into the dining room and garden in the other. Fittings are simple and solid, slotted into giant slabs of concrete.

2

3

2. The main stair intrudes very little into the tall and spacious dining room. It is the only decoration that this wall needs.
3. Abstract views throughout the house are the equivalent of abstract modern canvases: this is a glimpse of a New Modern house as a work of inhabitable modern art.

Highly visible, open stairs punctuate the New Modern interior, creating spatial drama.

ROGERS' HOUSE
LONDON, ENGLAND
RICHARD ROGERS

1. A lightweight steel stair criss-crosses its way up through the open interior of the house. The stair has become not just a way of connecting different levels, but a powerful visual device.

The drama of the stair

2. The experience of this spidery walkway is not one for those with a fear of heights. But even vertigo sufferers can admire the engineering verve that has gone into this radical reappraisal of the domestic stair.

In any house of any architectural distinction in any country and no matter what period, stairs have always been more than a functional means of climbing from one floor to another. The structure of a stair has always seemed dramatic, while the symbolic role of the stair has only been denied in the cheapest, poorest or meanest homes. The staircase probably reached its most dramatic expression in the Mannerist and Baroque palaces of 16th and 17th century Italy. Nevertheless, industrial materials developed during the 19th century gave a new drama to stairs, and one that Modern architects and engineers have continued to experiment with throughout the 20th century.

The drama of the perforated iron stair was shown to vertiginous advantage in Gustav Eiffel's famous tower built for the Paris Exhibition of 1889. New materials and a radically new approach to interior planning gave architects a new excuse to play high games with stairs from the 1920s. Some, like Frank Lloyd Wright in the design of the Guggenheim Museum, New York, went so far as to ban the stair altogether, replacing it with spiralling ramps. Le Corbusier, too, employed ramps as well as sweeping, streamlined stairways in his early white houses such as the Villa Stein (1926–7) or the Villa Savoie (1928–9) in France. The escalator added further drama to the interiors of public buildings. The new Lloyds' headquarters in the City of London (1981–6), designed by Richard Rogers

1

2

TSAO APARTMENT
NEW YORK, USA
TSAO-MCKOWN

1. New Modern interiors open up all sorts of possibilities for games of abstraction and visual tricks. Here, a delicate spiral stair appears to climb through the space normally reserved for a picture above the fireplace.

TOWN HOUSE
SURREY, ENGLAND
PIERRE D'AVOINE ARCHITECTS

2. The way out to the roof terrace of this town house is clearly marked by a custom-made matte-black steel stair. What might have been a utilitarian appendage has been treated as a surprising work of functional sculpture.
3. Detail of the sheet steel stair leading to the roof terrace. The design implies a traditional folding rooflight stair, but the architects have made a virtue from functional necessity. Its cut-away profile also allows maximum daylight.

& Partners, and the Hong Kong headquarters for the Hong Kong Shanghai Bank (1981–6), by Foster Associates, show how custom-designed escalators climbing silently at gentle angles through lofty, glazed atria have much the same impact as the great Baroque stairways of the past.

But the type of Modern stair that really caught modern architects' and designers' imagination was the gently spiralling stair climbing up through a glass tower. Walter Gropius, founder of the Bauhaus, made a very early use of this device in the model factory he built for the Deutsche Werkbund exhibition at Cologne, Germany in 1914. The device became a powerful Modern movement icon. The German architect Erich Mendelsohn (1888-1957), who worked in the United States, England and Palestine as well as his native Germany, created some of the most memorable of these stairs in his designs for the streamlined Shocken department stores in Germany and in the delightful De La Warr Pavilion (1935–6) at Bexhill-on-Sea, England. One of the earliest and most influential domestic uses of the steel stair running in a tight spiral up through a glazed stairwell in a distinctly Modern interior was at 'E1027,' the house that the Irish architect Eileen Gray built for herself at Roquebrune, France between 1926 and 1929.

The Modern stair not only developed a drama very much of its own as architects experimented with new forms and materials but, as in the great Renaissance houses of Europe, it sometimes became the most important decorative device in an interior. Certainly this is true of the perforated steel stair that connects the various levels of Richard and Ruth Rogers' house in Chelsea, London, England (see page 38). The lightness and the almost transparent qualities of such a stair mean that, although having a dramatic impact, it takes up precious little space. In smaller houses than the Rogers,' lightweight stairs free what might otherwise be wasted, gloomy or redundant space. Thus, the stair in the Gallery house, London (see page 49), a quietly dramatic set piece in a sculptural interior, takes up very little room.

The design of the stairs themselves is of particular importance in a New Modern house in which the interior is essentially open-plan or in which living spaces flow one into another. When the stair is on display it needs to be well-detailed. But because flexibility is the key-note of a New Modern interior, a stairway can be as tightly or as generously planned as is considered necessary. In the twin houses designed by David Wild (see page 46) the treatment of the stairs in one of the interiors is very different from the other. One of the houses is a family home that places a premium on living and bedroom space, so here Wild has devised a compact dog-leg stair that takes up less room than a stair in any conventional developers' house. But in the second house, designed for a single person given to entertaining at home, the stair takes on a grand and processional impact. Instead of being hidden away in the walls, it climbs up through the house in full view.

The importance of the stair shown in the houses illustrated in these pages reveals how New Modern design has broken away from the idea of the stair as a basic means of getting from one floor to another. Instead, it has turned what was a functional necessity into what is often the single most decorative device in the home.

3

1

2

3

TOWN HOUSE
SURREY, ENGLAND
PIERRE D'AVOINE ARCHITECTS

1. In small town houses the New Modern architect creates the illusion of space. These two stairways suggest generous space in a very small envelope of bricks and mortar, while the imaginative detailing is an unexpected bonus.
2 & 3. Cluttered decorative detail can steal much-needed living and breathing space in a small house. Here the architect has taken the end of a stair and its balustrade and transformed it into a decorative, yet decidedly functional artwork.

2

WYCHCOMBE STUDIOS
LONDON, ENGLAND
RICK MATHER ARCHITECTS

1. The spiral stair is the obvious and age-old way of climbing up through a house without sacrificing much-needed living space. Here this timeless device is given a fresh twist, with a tubular steel balustrade that adds its own sculptural drama.
2. In the New Modern house, the stair is a prominent and well-lit feature, as here, and not hidden away as in many traditionally planned houses. Steel, tubular and meshed, highlights this sense of lightness.
3. Exciting shapes and patterns are formed by the stair as it spirals against a background of shifting architectural forms, although here this abstraction is softened by the blue carpet of the treads.

1

1

WILD HOUSE
LONDON, ENGLAND
DAVID WILD

1. Here, the dog-leg stair – a typical feature of old London terraced houses – is brought up to date to save space, which has been given over to living and bedrooms. Grand processional stairs are more elegant, but occupy much-needed space in city plots.

2

PRIVATE RESIDENCE
LONDON, ENGLAND
DAVID WILD

2. The structure of each step is clearly on show. This arrangement not only imparts a sense of lightness to New Modern homes, but also appears to increase space when this is at a premium, as in this small city house.

POWER STATION HOUSE
TEXAS, USA
GARY CUNNINGHAM

3. Built into an old power station, the stair that winds up through this Texan house draws its imagery from industry. Steel handrails and translucent glass side panels lead up from a concrete base. But because this is a house, the treads are of warm, rich wood.

3

2

GAREY HOUSE
CONNECTICUT, USA
GWATHMEY SIEGEL

1. Echoing the Modern houses of the 1920s and 1930s, New Modern homes make frequent use of nautical imagery – panelling, ship's railings and bulkhead lamps, in the case of this stairwell.

TOWN HOUSE
LONDON, ENGLAND
NICHOLAS GRIMSHAW

2. Glass panels protect this stair edge. The panels are held in place by highly visible cast iron brackets. Such exposure of functional details requires a very high standards of workmanship.

3

4

GALLERY HOUSE
LONDON, ENGLAND
CHASSAY AND WILSON

3. The beautifully made stair climbing up against a pure white backdrop is meant to make you wonder exactly how it manages to stay up. It is intended to be a surrealist sculpture in its own right, a play with the idea of house as modern art gallery.

TOWN HOUSE
SURREY, ENGLAND
PIERRE D'AVOINE ARCHITECTS

4. This stair makes optimum use of very restricted space in a small town house. Although the house was a low-cost project, because the stair is a prominent feature, the architects have spent wisely on warm wood and well-crafted joinery.

1

2

NICK KNIGHT HOUSE
SURREY, ENGLAND
DAVID CHIPPERFIELD

1 & 2. In a house with three distinct stairs, this is the most conventional. In solid wood, it links bedrooms, bathroom and studio with the ground floor living room. The cut-away – matched by the projecting stairs below – allows glimpses, descending the stair, into the living room and garden beyond.

1

1 & 2. This small, space-saving stair gives access to a roof terrace. To the left of the stair is a bridge connecting the bedrooms and bathroom. Throughout the house, changes of level, flights of stairs and structural cut-aways link the various spaces together (see pp. 50–1).

Mezzanines allow double-height rooms to be divided without losing their clarity or stealing space. They make exciting places to sleep or play.

Mezzanine levels

New Modern houses are open houses, often crystal clear in conception and plan. Unlike traditional houses, they are not divided up into a labyrinth of small rooms and, for the most part, long, narrow space-wasting corridors have been abandoned. In a New Modern house spaces are connected by large openings instead of small doors, by exposed stairs and bridges across voids. One of the most characteristic of these connecting spaces is the mezzanine or gallery.

A mezzanine floor that opens at one end to a double-height room has several advantages over a conventional intermediate floor. First, it is dramatic, allowing views through and out of a house as if from the top of a ladder. Second, because it is open at one end it can be low-ceilinged without inducing claustrophobia. This means that a mezzanine floor can be inserted into a room or space that is less than the height of two conventional floors. Third, it animates the interior of a house – there is something intangibly attractive about seeing activities going on at several levels at once. This is much the same kind of "buzz" that we get from seeing people at work or play on several decks of an ocean liner.

Best of all, the mezzanine floor imparts a generous sense of space. In the small houses designed by Pierre D'Avoine in Richmond-upon-Thames, Surrey, England (see page 63), the mezzanine floors that house bedrooms and bathrooms look out over double-height living spaces. So although the bedrooms in these houses are smaller than they might have been, the living spaces are considerably larger, brighter and more welcoming than the purchasers of an inexpensive house in a London suburb would normally expect. Rather than spreading a number of small to medium-sized rooms through these houses, D'Avoine has chosen instead to make certain rooms small and one disproportionately large. The effect is one of generosity. The assumption is that every house or apartment should have at least one large room. This is the opposite of the early German Modern Movement's *Existenzminimum* thinking, whereby it was assumed that working-class families needed no more than functional rooms in which to rest and to prepare for the next day's toil in the new factories.

In strictly architectural terms, the effect of walking through a sequence of small rooms under

2

PRIVATE RESIDENCE
LONDON, ENGLAND
DAVID WILD

1, 2 & 3. The double-height space inside this house is revealed from the outside: the balcony represents the mezzanine level (above). The same space from the front of house is marked by a giant window (right). Inside, the mezzanine itself provides views into each corner of the house. Its course is interrupted by the dramatic structural columns of the house and by the polished stainless steel chimney flue (far right).

3

2

fairly low ceilings into a lofty space, perhaps divided by a gallery or mezzanine, is an exciting one. When space is at a premium, as in most cities, this architectural device is doubly welcome. The effect is shown to advantage in different ways in the twin houses that David Wild has designed in London's Camden Town. In the family house, Wild has packed the stair, bedrooms and bathrooms into relatively small areas. The space thus saved has been used to create an impressive double-height living room that could only otherwise belong to a much larger and infinitely more expensive house. In the adjoining house, the architect has opened up a large, double-height living space spanned by a steel mezzanine. Here, the effect has been to create a distinctly public domain within a private house; the mezzanine adds theatrical impact to a house in which entertaining has been placed at a premium.

1, 2 & 3. Mezzanines can be seen as a luxury as they occupy only a small area of what could be a complete floor. Their virtue is that they break up the volume of a house, bringing various spaces into common view and encouraging daylight throughout the house (above). Here, the austere structure of the mezzanine is offset by the luxurious use of black-veined marble for the fireplace and of highly reflective stainless steel for the chimney flue.

1 & 2. The mezzanine floor is reached via the main stair, which, as seen here, runs down to face the black marble monolith of the fireplace. Each element of this house, mezzanine included, is quite clearly separate, and even made from distinctive materials, yet they all connect to form a gently dramatic whole. The open form of the stairs means that rooms, spaces and details of the house are gradually revealed as people climb up, down and through the building. Here, the stair meets the dining room sited underneath the mezzanine.

2

Previous page. The dining area sits protected under the mezzanine bridge and behind the black marble fireplace. This arrangement heightens the scale of the double-height living space. It also ensures a change in the tone and intensity of daylight passing through the large front window.

1

2

BARNES APARTMENT
LONDON, ENGLAND
MUNKENBECK & MARSHALL

1. The polished wood mezzanine acts as a sleeping platform, with a further mezzanine bridge, separately identified by its gridded steel structure, leading out and onto the roof.

WYCHCOMBE STUDIOS
LONDON, ENGLAND
RICK MATHER ARCHITECTS

2. A sweeping, Le Corbusier-inspired stair leads up to a mezzanine bridge that links the large double-height living room to other rooms. Flooring materials change as the mezzanine gives way to the next floor.

3

TOWN HOUSE
SURREY, ENGLAND
PIERRE D'AVOINE ARCHITECTS

3. The mezzanine arrangement in this small London suburban house has been designed to allow a generous double-height living room. The architect decided to offer residents more living space rather than what would otherwise be an extra, cramped bedroom.

New Modern homes make the most of daylight. Free-flowing spaces and unexpected windows create poetic effects of light and shade.

The mastery of light

1

The cult of sunbathing, the infatuation with sun and light that first found a place in sophisticated western lifestyles during the 1920s encouraged an appropriate architecture. And new developments in glass, if not necessarily in insulation, encouraged the use of giant picture windows. For generations brought up in dark and musty Victorian houses, picture windows, uninterrupted views and sunlight could only be at a premium. Balconies designed to resemble the sun decks of ocean liners became fashionable in the 1920s. Open-plan interiors allowed the sun to penetrate the deepest recesses of the Modern interior.

The New Modern interior is not so slavish to the cult of sun worship. Now that sunbathing itself has proved to be dangerous rather than life-enhancing, the obsession with maximum light levels has declined. In the dogmatically Modern house of the 1920s through to the 1970s, light levels always had to be at a maximum. In a typical Modern or modernized family house of the 1970s, found anywhere from the Californian coast to the forests of southern Germany, kitchens would be flooded in light from a high-powered fluorescent tube; bedrooms, living rooms and bathrooms were

2

KIDOSAKI HOUSE
TOKYO, JAPAN
TADAO ANDO

1. The geometry of a New Modern house encourages a sophisticated play of light, here enhanced by sunshine filtering through a tree.
2. Trees, recessed doorway, and stairs modulate daylight flooding into this courtyard.
3. The harshness of the concrete walls is offset by the play of light in the courtyard, as well as by the relationship between the trees and daylight. The Japanese idea of an external room (see page 171) is also seen here.
4. Utter simplicity is the keynote of this Ando house. Daylight, mingled with the delicate, gently moving shadows cast by the trees in the courtyard beyond, pours through the dining room window into this chaste concrete and wooden chamber. This highlights the beautifully jointed floor as well as the accurately cast concrete walls. It also emphasises the ship's prow shape of the custom-designed dining table.

At night, curtainless, the window becomes like a dark canvas, while precisely directed electric light pinpoints the main features of the statuary.

3

4

frazzled under batteries of hot, swivel-mounted spotlights, while bathrooms resembled the interiors of refrigerators. It has taken a long time for this obsession with sun and light to die down.

The New Modern interior demands light, both natural and artificial, but in more subtle ways and quantities. The first question a New Modern architect or householder should ask is where do I want light and why do I want it there? How can I make the best use of light? Several of the houses shown in this book make particularly subtle use of daylight. Stairwells in the middle of small, tightly planned city houses and apartments, for example, have been top lit when capped with a flat roof. This simple expedient completely transforms a stair that is best placed in what would otherwise be a dingy location. The New Modern designer aims to optimize rather than maximize the use and play of light.

In the house John Pawson and Claudio Silvestrin have designed in London, England (see pages 70–5), light is brought gently into the living room through translucent floor-to-ceiling screens. On the other side of the house light enters through windows that allow selected views out and romantic chutes of light in to fall across the beautiful wood floor of the hallway. This is perhaps the greatest difference between the way architects and designers used daylight until a decade or so ago and the way that they are beginning to use it now. Light is there to be modulated, to create poetic effects in interior spaces, as well as to illuminate.

The picture window was a reaction to gloomy interiors rather than to traditional windows themselves. But in their quest for light the post-Victorian generations threw the glazing bar out with the old window. The subtlety of framed views gave way to panoramic views, in the same way that the magic lantern had yielded to "cinemascope" screens. Many traditional houses have been spoilt by the intrusion of giant picture windows, while an equal number of Modern houses have suffered dazzling interiors for the same reason. The houses illustrated in this book show how the best use of views and daylight can be made without resort to excessive glazing. The overprovision of glazing in many Modern buildings has often led to absurd wastage of energy: energy, for example, needed to keep houses cool in summer and warm in winter.

The aim of the architect in designing a New Modern house is to distribute light and air without wasting energy, while at the same time creating poetic effects or painting with light.

Beyond the window, other areas are explored: a play of daylight can be made through the use of materials and colors chosen for surfaces, stairs and furniture. Metal surfaces catch and reflect light; so do white walls. And white walls can be enriched by a play of shadows.

A second great change wrought by the New Moderns has been in the use of artificial light. The sheer range of sophisticated domestic lighting now on the market makes virtually any kind or degree of lighting available. Electric light can be warm or cold; used to wash a room with light or directed with pin-point accuracy on a painting or object. Sources of ambient light can be completely hidden, with pools of romantic or purposeful task lighting available from any number of sources, from candelabras to anglepoise lamps.

A New Modern interior has no need to show off the technology of electric lighting. Sources might be concealed, while switches can now be very discreet. It is an irony, in traditional houses, to celebrate the humble light switch. And yet highly decorative gilt switches sell in vast numbers. So too do an excessive number of lamps which serve only to clutter an interior. Even at the beginning of the 1990s very few specialist lighting designers and few architects seem trained to do more than the obvious with sources of artificial light. Among the proliferation of modern lamps there are only a small number of new classics, such as Richard Sapper's *Tizio* lamp, that rank along with the finest lamps of the past. The most useful modern lamps are the small, low-voltage fittings that can be set into ceilings to provide light with the minimum of disruption to the esthetic of any interior.

1. Daylight passes into the Kidosaki house from the most oblique sources. The sculptures and free-standing objects are inescapably on show and so need to be impressive, striking or just well-made. In this case, they are all three.

2. A window in the wall demonstrates how New Modern architecture, in sharp contrast with conventional house design, is as much to do with the play of light and shade as it is with the logic of its interiors or with generous use of space.

A striking example of how daylight can provide all the play and variation in a room that we normally demand from pictures, carpets, fabrics and decorative objects. Throughout the day, light effects change – furniture and objects graduating from stark two-dimensional to rich three-dimensional qualities.

1

MINIMALIST HOUSE
LONDON, ENGLAND
PAWSON AND SILVESTRIN

1 & 2. Light filters into this hallway from four distinct sources: through windows backed by fine venetian blinds (seen at the far right hand side of the hall); through living room windows protected by translucent glass screens (offstage right through the passageway); through the clear kitchen windows (offstage, passageway left) and from the lights mounted under the hallway's wooden floor. The net effect is one of great subtlety and one that can be manipulated throughout the day. The corridor shown on the right is lit more directly by sunlight pouring through venetian blinds and top lighting from the bedrooms located on the floor above.

2

The living room is lit during the day by sunlight passing through translucent glass screens mounted in front of the windows facing the street. This creates an atmosphere of calm, even in a noisy city. At night, lights fixed behind the screens transform the character of the room, but it remains equally tranquil.

1 & 2. The effect of daylight passing through one of the two milky glass screens into the dining area (left) is quite magical, yet is achieved through a device of the utmost simplicity. Such simplicity is both hard for designers to reach and for their clients to come to terms with – until they see the final effect, as here. It is possible to walk behind the screens into the original window alcoves to feel reconnected with the bustling world outside (right).

2

1

2

MURPHY HOUSE
CALIFORNIA, USA
BRIAN MURPHY

1. This Californian house is a play on old colonial and New Modern themes. The harsh sunlight creates sharp shadows, but daylight is softened and distorted through a number of devices: pool, balconies, awnings, porches and the external spiral stair.
2. Plain white surfaces might seem less intriguing than bricks, timbers and stone – at least at the design stage of a new house – but the reality can be very different. Brian Murphy has modulated light and shade to the advantage of this cool, white house.
3. The disciplined, yet free-flowing plan of this house makes decorative use of daylight. Here sunlight is seen creating imaginary floor and wall coverings. The airiness of this breezy dining room is enhanced by pools of light rippling in the hallway and in the room lit from above to the left. Lightweight furniture makes the most of warm Californian sunlight, yet the lessons can be applied in other climates and in smaller spaces.

3

1

2

1. The contrast between light and shade is emphasized in the choice of furniture and decoration. The matte black of rug, firegrate and lamp bases offsets the crisp whiteness of walls, ceilings, chairs and paintwork. This contrast is underlined by the checkerboard pattern of windows, fireplace and doors set in the wall. Light is brought into the house through glazed doors, as well as windows. Internal doors are glazed too, to diffuse light throughout the house.

2. Building a New Modern house does not mean having to abandon the lessons of traditional construction. A New Modern house can be built of mud, clay and wattle, steel or concrete. It is the plan and play of light that separates it from earlier traditions of housebuilding. These simple light baffles, made from branches and twigs, are both sculptural and effective in keeping the midday sun at bay. They also create playful patterns of light on exterior and interior surfaces.

1

1. The black massing of the grand piano responds to the filigree forms of the white-painted wrought-iron screen above it – just one of the many calculated juxtapositions of black on white in this house. This view shows just how many shades of white there can be when light, whether daylight or artificial, is carefully planned.

2

2. On view is the full effect of daylight on screens, light-wells and slatted furniture. The lack of walls compounds the effect. Only New Modern free-flowing space allows such a symphony of light. In a conventional house, the plan of which is composed of small, box-like rooms, daylight is not given a chance to sing like this. In gloomier climates, where sunshine is not guaranteed, a related effect can be achieved with the subtle use of sophisticated electric lighting fitments.

3. The manipulation of sunlight in the Murphy house stems not just from the louvers and baffles that diminish its intensity, but also from the considered forms of the architecture. Light-wells such as this one have been calculated for their effect on light, ventilation and the overall look of the building. As in all New Modern houses, the creation of abstract forms is both a formal game and a functional response to the needs of climate, accommodation and building technology.

3

2

3

SHINOHARA HOUSE
TOKYO, JAPAN
PROFESSOR SHINOHARA

1. Planes of light on the walls contrast with the dappled light effects animating the tiled floor. Framed views of surrounding nature are on offer. There is a deliberate contrast between the yielding forms of the trees outside and the ungiving arithmetic of the architecture. In this room it is possible to contemplate natural surroundings without distraction from man-made artefacts.
2. Outside, the design of the house is much more in harmony with its natural surroundings. Organic shapes replace right angles and give in readily to natural light and shade.
3. The light effects here play several games. The angled window, cut away at a steep rake, creates a marked difference in the quality of light on the walls, while making the view outside look like a painting hung on a gallery wall.

1

BJORNSEN HOUSE
LOS ANGELES, USA
ARATA ISOSAKI

1 & 2. Venetian blinds control daylight, modulate the otherwise unrelieved whiteness of walls and appear as a simple work of sculpture in their own right. In this kitchen-diner a daylight effect is provided at night by exposed fluorescent tubes.

2

3

WYCHCOMBE STUDIOS
LONDON, ENGLAND
RICK MATHER ARCHITECTS

3. Roller blinds are a simple and effective way of curbing excessive sunlight, while casting ever-changing patterns on walls and floor. Without these, summer sunlight would be harsh and ungiving, even in England. In winter, excess light is no problem. The blind's role becomes one of insulation – they will prevent heat escaping.

BJORNSEN HOUSE
LOS ANGELES, USA
ARATA ISOSAKI

4. The dining room, with its internal windows, appears to be in a separate house looking through a second, with a third beyond. The net effect of this is a complex and subtle play of daylight: pools of light and shade and much variation in the colour and intensity of light. Fluorescent tubes fixed high in the gallery recreate daylight at night.

2

SPIELBERG HOUSE
LONG ISLAND, USA
GWATHMEY SEIGEL

1. Here a simple use of shutters over the clerestory windows has the effect of drawing daylight into the lower half of the room only. On a hot day this ensures that the room is bathed and not bleached by sunlight. The blonde wood floor makes the most of light washing into the house at this low angle.
2. In this view daylight is seen slanting down from the upper windows, making the simple wood chair glow and bringing the old timbers out of the shadows. The sheer volume of light makes this house different from its traditional counterparts, from which it takes its esthetic cues. However, as in all New Modern designs, light is carefully controlled.

1

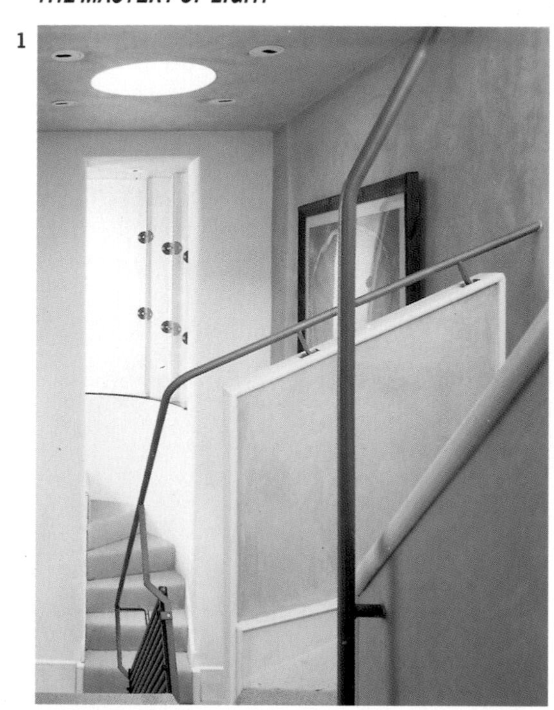

2

3

BARNES APARTMENT
LONDON, ENGLAND
MUNKENBECK & MARSHALL

1. Light-wells punched through flat roofs bring daylight cascading down stairs.

OPEL HOUSE
VERMONT, USA
GWATHMEY SEIGEL

2. Daylight enters this studio-study through a wall of glass bricks, windows and a light-well.

WILD HOUSE
LONDON, ENGLAND
DAVID WILD

3 & 4. Light is used in this hallway to create a pattern of solids and voids. What could be an austere room is relieved by light reflecting from the polished terrazzo floor and by the variety of angles in which light is brought into play.

At night the New Modern house glows with light. Its innate transparency is shown to magical effect as the sky begins to darken.

New Modernism at night

GAREY HOUSE
CONNECTICUT, USA
GWATHMEY SIEGEL

The Garey House is a lighthouse at night; the triple-height central drum that forms the principal living spaces is entirely exposed to the outside world without so much as a gossamer-thin curtain to protect the occupants from prying eyes. But its private setting ensures that the only lookers-on will be owls and animal nightlife.

Before the advent of electricity, the night belonged to any number of chronicled ghosts and unknown demons. And the demonology of the night was all the more terrifying for its all too real cut-throats, thugs and villains. Houses were sealed up at sunset, shades drawn, shutters bolted across windows, candles, oil lamps and fires lit. The wiles of man and nature, as well as damp and drafts, were, to an extent, successfully shut out until sunrise.

Modern technology and methods of construction appear to have changed all this. Less so perhaps in the most violent areas of modern cities, but certainly in suburbs, small towns and the countryside. With effective insulation and draft-free windows, with light and warmth available at the touch of a switch, the idea of huddling inside a house has lost some of its hold. People still love to sit around the hearth, but warm inside a Modern house nature seems less of a threat. In fact, the best contemporary Modern houses open up to the night in a way that would have once seemed as unlikely as it would have been undesirable.

The Opel House (see pages 92–3), designed by Charles Gwathmey, is a perfect example of how a New Modern house is responsive to nature both during the day and at night. The view out across the lake from the living room is impressive at any time, but as night descends it is quite beautiful. Charles Gwathmey's touch of genius is to have set a fireplace in what is otherwise a wall of glass. On the coldest nights of the year nature can be watched at work while sitting around a blazing fire. In traditional houses the fireplace would never be set on an exterior wall in this fashion. The conventional idea of sitting around the fire has always involved

1

2

OPEL HOUSE
VERMONT, USA
GWATHMEY SIEGEL

1. Unusually, the fireplace is set on the external wall of the living room. At dusk this architectural gamesmanship is seen to full advantage. Sitting here, the owners enjoy the best of both worlds: a view of both the lake and a blazing fire.

2. Interior view of the exterior in picture 3. By setting the fire surround into a frame of glass bricks, Charles Gwathmey has emphasized the symbolic role of the hearth.

3. A view from the garden into a living room at night. The chimney flue divides the facade into a studied plane of geometrical abstracts.

3

turning your back to the windows and the vagaries of the night. Gwathmey, as only a New Modern is prepared to do today, has turned convention on its head and in doing so added to the serenity of a house that intrudes gently into its untamed setting.

In cities, however, the night is still as threatening as it has always been. Except for those who live in a well-secured apartment block, today's city dwellers feel the same need as their pre-electric ancestors to shut themselves away from the all too familiar threats outside. But often this is achieved without the use of conventional shutters, shades or curtains. In a strikingly minimalist house designed by John Pawson and Claudio Silvestrin in London, England (see pages 70–5), night is banished altogether from the living room. Here, massive opaque glass screens have been placed behind the windows. During the day sunlight filters through, creating a peaceful and calm interior that might be miles from the hustle of the city. At night, ceiling lights set between the windows and the screens repeat what the sun does by day. In this way the living room enjoys the same serene ambience whatever the hour. It is a clever conceit, a new and modern way of thinking about the lighting of a room. It is also a device that creates a mid-way light that is neither quite day or quite night – a timeless zone.

By night, New Modern children enjoy the psychological security of their houses. A house without spooky corridors and worrysome staircases is easy on a child's impressionable mind. The openness of a New Modern house takes away at least some of the stuff that nightmares are made of. By nature sociable and inviting, modern houses create a sense of well-being. They are not for people for whom gloom, shadows and creaking floorboards are a delight.

4

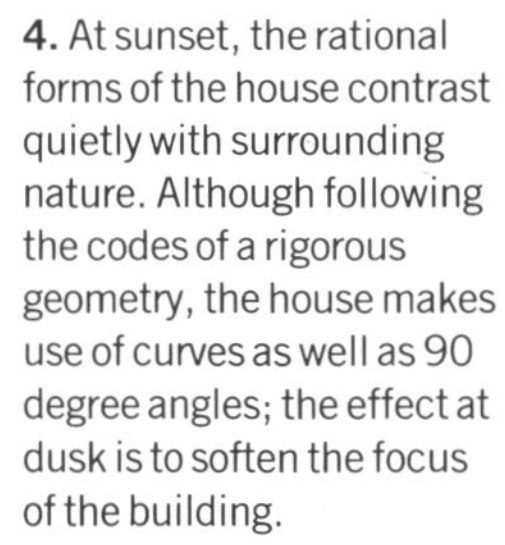

4. At sunset, the rational forms of the house contrast quietly with surrounding nature. Although following the codes of a rigorous geometry, the house makes use of curves as well as 90 degree angles; the effect at dusk is to soften the focus of the building.

SPIELBERG HOUSE
LONG ISLAND, USA
GWATHMEY SIEGEL

At first glance this house looks quite conventional, yet as the sun goes down and the lights come on it reveals a subtle play between old tradition and new modernity. The light shining through the skylight lets you know that all is not as it seems: modern design has been gently at work. Modern exterior lighting also plays a role, tracing magical patterns across the lake.

2

1

KIDOSAKI HOUSE
TOKYO, JAPAN
TADAO ANDO

1. One of the ideas governing the design of Japanese houses is that of the outside room (see p. 171). In this view of the Kidosaki house the night sky forms a deep blue ceiling over the extended concrete frame of the building. The view from this outside "room" into the kitchen and bedroom is a play of mathematical forms.

2. At night, the Kadosaki house looks as if the owners have peeled away the walls to let passers-by see the rigorous, necessarily immaculate, yet warm simplicity of its interior. The generous windows make the most of sunlight during the day, while at night a sophisticated use of electric light creates its own special and varied effects.

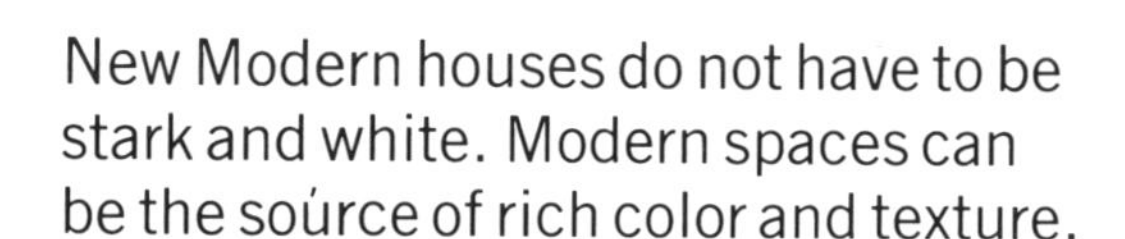

New Modern houses do not have to be stark and white. Modern spaces can be the soúrce of rich color and texture.

Color and texture

When the initial wave of recognizably Modern architecture first appeared in European magazines in the 1920s, illustrations were necessarily in black and white. Radical young architects in Britain and the United States studied these magazines and got the wrong impression of Modern interiors. They imagined that they were as insistently white as they appeared to be on the page. Nothing could have been further from the truth. While it was true that achromatic white was predominant in the new houses and apartments of Germany and France in the 1920s, chromatic color was also of great importance. In Le Corbusier's early Modern villas of the 1920s, such as Villa Savoie, Poissy, France, color was used to dramatic effect. In the absence of wallpaper, panelling or decorative surface treatments, Corbusier would have whole walls of his *machines à habiter* painted in bright hues. In fact, Corbusier interiors are remarkable for their dramatic use of vivid colors. In contemporary photographs, however, these showed up as different shades of white, off-white and gray.

The more International Modern houses and apartments from the 1920s and 1930s you visit, the more you realise just how important a factor chromatic color was. Even so, white remains the essential backdrop to Modern and New Modern living. The reasons are not hard to find, although they sound odd perhaps in the 1990s. After the carnage of the First World War, architects seized on white because it was clinical and pure. White was the color of the sanitorium, of nurses' starched uniforms, of a fresh start. After the Great War continental European architects attempted to make a clean break from pre-war design. They abandoned heavily decorated, richly colored, plushly garbed interior styles in pursuit of a new purity. Not surprisingly, some of the most successful and endearing European buildings of the 1920s are, in fact, not houses but sanitoria, exemplified by Alvar Aalto's hugely influential tuberculosis sanitorium in Paimio, Finland, begun in 1929.

2

1

TSAO APARTMENT
NEW YORK, USA
TSAO-MCKOWN

1. The use of color in this apartment is vibrant, yet in accord with New Modern thinking. Color is used in blocks: a column of red, a plane of mauve.
2. Here the differing textures of natural and man-made materials are juxtaposed.

The design of this bedroom is simple, yet sumptuous. The effect is won through the generous scale of the bed and the warm texture of the polished wood floor: fitted carpet never evokes this sense of luxury. Translucent fabric screens at the bed ends and delicate, semi-sheer curtains breathe a sensual atmosphere into the room.

But white was much more than this. It was also the color adopted for millenia by builders and architects on either side of the Mediterranean. White was necessary to keep the sun at bay, to prevent houses from heating up during the day. In the 1920s and 1930s the cult of sun-worship was adopted throughout Europe and the United States. Architects began to design white houses even in such changeable climes as England. This was an architecture of optimism. It was also the architecture of hygiene. When Europe and the United States were still heavily industrialized and before clean air legislation began to remove excessive soot from the skies, cities were sulfurous places. To paint a house white was an act of faith, a fight against filth, disease and squalor. White had been used like this before. In Regency London white-painted stucco was all the rage. The picturesque and theatrical villas and terraces John Nash and his associates designed and built around Regent's Park in the 1820s still gleam agelessly after every fresh lick of paint. Given the squalor of the period they must have seemed a glimpse of Arcadia. They still do.

White has also long been the color chosen by iconoclasts. It was chosen by the crusaders to take their less-than-holy fight to the Holy Land. It was used by Protestants throughout Europe to overpaint the walls of richly decorated Catholic churches at the time of the Reformation. Not surprisingly, it was the dominant color on the palette of revolutionary Modern Movement architects after the First World War.

Today, these aspects of white are at most subliminal, although clients with a passion for cleanliness and order still choose white as the predominant color for their interiors. The American architect Richard Meier still refuses to deviate from the principle of the white house. His brilliant, abstract New England houses stand like modern temples in the lush and provident American landscape.

White remains the best background against which to show off abstract Modern as well as historic furniture and design. Modern furniture has often been designed to provoke as well as to serve a practical purpose. It has often been used as a means of exploring new design ideas. A chair such as Gerrit Rietveld's Red and Blue chair of 1918 was designed, like an abstract Modern painting, to stand alone. As a one-off piece that is unlikely

1

1. A meeting of planes and corrugations of timber, chintz, silk, terrazzo, bronze, brass, glass and plaster. This is colorful proof of the fact that New Modern interiors can make full use of the decorator's palette.

2. With their clear forms and precise use of color, New Modern interiors act as showcases for contemporary objects, highlighting such extremes as artwork, a sculpture here, to everyday objects like these shoes.

to bear any relationship to other pieces of furniture in the same room, it is seen to best advantage standing apart against a white background. Only then can its bold and colorful abstract geometry make sense.

Purist modern architects such as Richard Meier or Rick Mather (see page 44) remain committed to white. Some, such as Claudio Silvestrin and John Pawson (see pages 70–5), argue that white is the most adaptable and subtle of all colors and have proved that it is possible to create a subtly changing mood in different parts of a mimimalist interior by applying white paint in several shades. Others, equally purist, such as David Wild, use white as a principal color, but offset with the bold use of planes of warm, rich hues. These architects would all agree that color and warmth in interiors is achieved first through the choice of building materials and the play of daylight and then through the selection of furniture, fittings and art. Traditional architects, designers and decorators believe differently and make their play for warmth and color through the rich use of fabrics, wallpapers, floor coverings and decorative objects.

Although any color is permissible in a New Modern interior, white remains the basis of decoration. The difference between the abstract Modern thinking and esthetic of the 1920s and 1930s and that of today is that the moral imperative for whiteness has gone. In times of esthetic revolutions designers work at extreme solutions, while in an eclectic age like ours design is less extreme. There is no one clear solution as there appeared to be to the leaders of the Modern Movement 70 years ago. White is not necessarily right. However, given that western societies are currently bombarded with design images not just from throughout the world but from throughout history, it is no small wonder that so many people are looking to white as a cleansing background in a world of visual clutter and color pollution.

2

3. At night the colors which seem so striking during daylight hours are mellowed, showing that color, texture, surfaces and light can be modified subtly to suit swings of mood and the time of day.

3. Soft, baggy, white fabric draped over simple black steel chair frames represent the essence of this highly individual apartment. Colours and textures are offset against each other, creating a complex visual dialogue that is not apparent at first.

CUBIST APARTMENT
NEW YORK, USA
STEVEN HOLL

1. The change in texture and color in this apartment is gradual. Shades and ploys of black and gray give way to yellow and white. Solid blocks of color are broken up into impressionist spots, dabs and speckles.
2. The square black and white terrazzo floor tiles frame the random edge of the painterly carpet. New Modern interiors provide a crisp, mathematical backdrop for organic shapes and forms, from chairs to carpets.

Machinery has often been garbed in the most glorious hues: think of railway locomotives or ocean liners, where functional artefacts obtain new depths through imaginative color schemes. Chromatic color is only deliberately excluded from New Modern houses when there are other agencies at work. In the examples of the Tokyo house by Tadao Ando (see page 64) and the Nick Knight house in Surrey, England (see page 32) color is provided by blossom and foliage, rather than by paint or dyes. However, in the case of the London house designed by John Pawson and Claudio Silvestrin (see page 70), white has made its unequivocal return. White suggests calm and rational order, while chromatic colors act as visual and emotional stimulants.

Certain 20th century architects working exclusively in a Modern idiom proved that a rich use of color could enhance their abstract designs. Perhaps the most remarkable Modern use of color is that made by the Mexican architect Luis Barragan, who died in 1988. Barragan found the work of most of his contemporaries too austere. In the speech he gave on receiving the prestigious American Priztker prize for architecture in 1980, he said, "To my dismay I have found that an alarming proportion of publications devoted to architecture have banished from their pages the words Beauty, Inspiration, Magic, Spellbound, Enchantment, as well as the concepts of Serenity, Silence, Intimacy and Amazement." He could have added color.

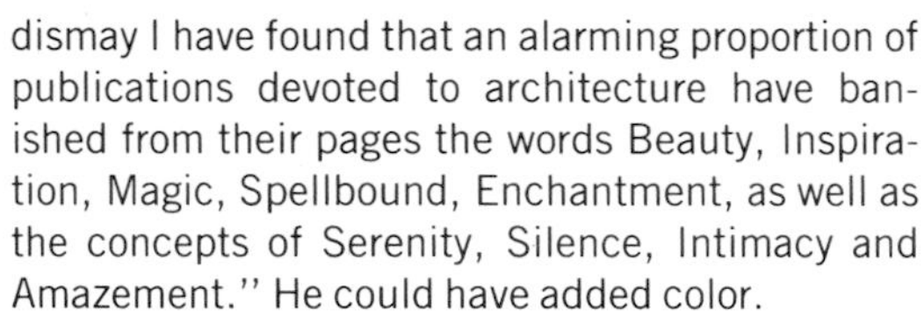

Barragan's buildings, fashionable once more, are a blaze of rich Mexican color – sundrenched ochres, reds, yellow and blues. Barragan's influence on New Modern designers and architects is strong, and will doubtless gather momentum. His work is proof that gorgeous color and Modernism need not inhabit separate worlds.

Just as Modern Movement houses of the 1920s, 1930s and 1940s were rarely as chaste in color as they appear in the black and white magazines of the period, so they were richer in texture. Adolf Loos, who worked in Vienna at the turn of the 20th century and was perhaps the founding father of the Modern house, campaigned vigorously against decoration, yet employed rich materials for both the structure and decoration of his houses. Fireplaces, bathrooms and floors might all be finished in expensive marbles. Woodwork, if plain, was of the highest possible quality. This theme continues in the houses of Le Corbusier in the 1920s. Smooth, white plastered walls might be the norm in houses by Corbusier and his contemporaries, but marble and wood were also used.

Modern houses inevitably generated their own design signature over the years, and many of these have been continued into the 1990s. New Modern houses are often characterized by highly polished and beautifully jointed wooden floors, by smoothly plastered walls and such luxuries as marble fire surrounds. Materials are used in what old Modern Movement architects described as an "honest" fashion: brass is brass, steel is steel and so on. This gives the best New Modern houses a purity and depth of texture. They should feel as solid and as tactile as an expensive piece of machinery.

1

2

Overleaf. The most important relationship this apartment has is to the craggy Manhattan skyline from which it draws its textured New Modern inspiration. Note the high-rise candlesticks which echo the form of classic skyscrapers.

New Modern houses are perfect foils to displays of contemporary art: some are designed as galleries.

The New Modern house as a gallery

1

BJORNSEN HOUSE
LOS ANGELES, USA
ARATA ISOZAKI

1. This New Modern house adopts the form of the traditional home; but the sheer volume of glass and its transparency are wholly new concerns.
2. The cactus has become a fashionable New Modern accessory. Here it adopts a role as sculpture, a foil to the severe geometry of the triangular skylight.
3. Not only is this full-height living room a gallery for paintings, sculpture and other artworks, but the end wall acts as a giant frame that sections off abstract views of the house beyond. Fine art is allowed to set the decorative agenda.

With surfaces largely free from decorative effects, the least significant object in a New Modern house is on display. In a cluttered country-house style interior, small busts and urns, clocks and miniatures, occasional chairs and valueless prints and paintings disappear into the crowd of color, fabrics, finishes and objects. The total effect given by the whole ensemble is what matters. Flaws in particular objects hardly matter when the net effect is one of artistic judgment, taste and grandeur, no matter how faded and worn.

2

But in a modern interior the opposite is true. One object out of place upsets the balance of the whole room. In this sense the New Modern path is a difficult one to tread. But then Modernism never has been an easy creed to follow. Modern architecture has failed so often because architects have been unable to accomodate its demanding nature. Each New Modern house or interior is a new opportunity, a blank canvas on which the architect and client can choose to do almost anything. Such freedom is an open invitation to errors of esthetic judgment. When minor architects and lesser builders worked to pattern books they were unlikely to go too far wrong. Modernism has been a demanding and difficult mistress.

It is especially problematic for the architect, client or decorator when considering the decoration of rooms. If these are meant to be purist then each piece of furniture, each painting, each decorative object has to be carefully considered. Filling a modern room or living space with a collection of intrinsically well-designed pieces is as likely to recreate the look of a furniture showroom as it is to create a successful domestic interior.

But this potential pitfall is also the great strength of a modern house. Because each object needs to be carefully considered, the New Modern has the chance of cutting down on domestic detritus, disposing of unwanted possessions.

Each object will be on display in much the same way as it is in an art gallery. The judicious placing of a few objects and a minimal amount of furniture might be just the right solution. Because even a compact modern house makes a generous use of space, that space and the freedom of movement it offers is best used to advantage and not given away to unwanted clutter.

This generosity of space allows New Moderns to indulge in large artworks that would not fit into a conventional house of the same size. A double-height living space means that you are free to hang a giant painting or move in a tall sculpture. Free from the dictates of historical precedent, you can move objects into living spaces that would be grossly misplaced in an old or mock-historic house. You can even contemplate a motorbike on the wall (see page 111).

For people with Modern art collections, Modern houses make particular sense. The Gallery house, London (see page 112), designed by Tchaik

S
E
X

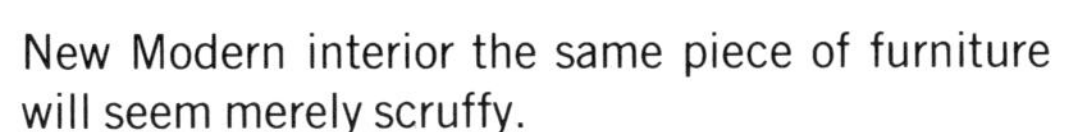

Chassay and Peter Wilson, is either an art gallery resembling a house or a house that makes a convincing art gallery. This particular art collection would seem out of place in a historic interior unless it was stripped to a bare shell. This is what Richard and Ruth Rogers have done to their own house in Chelsea, London. What appears to be a conventional late Georgian facade reveals a remarkable open-plan house in which massive artworks find a ready and convincing home. The Andy Warhol Chairman Mao prints that dominate one wall would look absurd without the generous white space around them. Because so much Modern art is deliberately unconventional, it is difficult to accommodate in conventional homes. Just as a Gainsborough looks best in an early classical English house, so a Warhol makes its greatest impact when free from immediate competition.

But the gallery-like quality of many New Modern interiors does mean that flaws in objects can be shown up to poor advantage. In a historic setting, a favorite, but worn and torn chair, for example, is best shown for what it is, its very raggedness treated as something to intrigue the eye. But in a New Modern interior the same piece of furniture will seem merely scruffy.

There are a number of architects and clients worldwide who believe that the purity of well-designed, chaste and beautifully built modern interiors should not be assailed by domestic clutter. They should be as minimal and as stark as an early mosque or Cistercian abbey. Finely joined wooden floors accompanied by white-painted plaster walls honed to perfection are in themselves adequate. This notion is too demanding for most people, yet it makes some sense. At their best, modern interiors can offer such generous space, even in small apartments and houses, that it seems a pity to lose any of that precious expanse by moving in furniture.

The Italian architect Claudio Silvestrin believes that the only way to ensure that a harmony remains between a purist interior and its decor is for the architect to design the accompanying furniture, preferably in the most permanent materials, stone among them. However, it must be said that, to some extent, this approach undermines the very notion of flexibility that New Modern interiors promise.

But the house as a gallery or else as a perfect, immutable art object in its own right is a luxury that few people can live with. Most people, families certainly, inevitably generate a certain amount of clutter. Only the most disciplined sensibility or domestic help will keep clutter wholly at bay. Nevertheless, the house as gallery has a role for people who live and work in cities. If you can eat all meals out and enjoy using the city to its fullest extent, the house as gallery makes sense. Although New Modern interiors do not need to be this exacting, the concept of the house as gallery is a reminder of how demanding – as well as how exciting and liberating – Modernism can be.

1. Living with contemporary art can be a demanding, if rewarding, experience. It requires real commitment to give over so much living space to a single sculpture, yet the effect is dramatic and compelling. This work is by Rauschenberg.

2. The internal end wall conceals both a door and several cupboards. The window of the dining room offers views into the gallery as if were exterior space.

3. Walls become floors or even pavement to park a MZ motorbike, otherwise a work by Mario Merz.

GALLERY HOUSE
LONDON, ENGLAND
CHASSAY AND WILSON

1. The Gallery house is tucked along a London mews between existing buildings. A giant window, an artwork in itself, is angled to attract attention as well as daylight.

2. Artworks are fully integrated into the structure of this domestic gallery, each element complementing the next. Daylight is encouraged into this lofty space through the main window to the mews as well as through a variety of shutes, slants and slots of varying sizes.

3. Furniture was specially commissioned for this house. Pieces were designed to be functional artworks, taking the idea of the house as art gallery to a logical and even practical conclusion. This marble-topped table is by the Glaswegian artist Bruce Maclean.

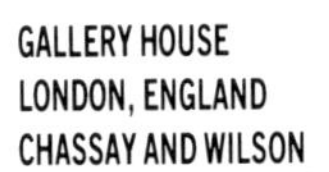

GALLERY HOUSE
LONDON, ENGLAND
CHASSAY AND WILSON

1. Each part of this house has been subsumed by contemporary art. Chairs, lamps and carpets are obvious contenders for the talents of artists and designers, yet here even windows have been commissioned.

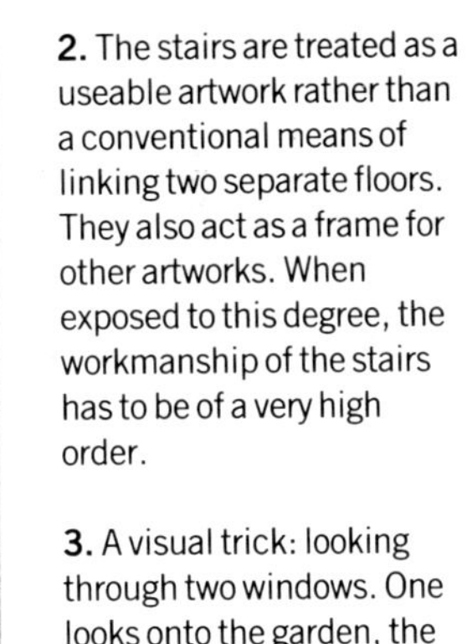

2. The stairs are treated as a useable artwork rather than a conventional means of linking two separate floors. They also act as a frame for other artworks. When exposed to this degree, the workmanship of the stairs has to be of a very high order.

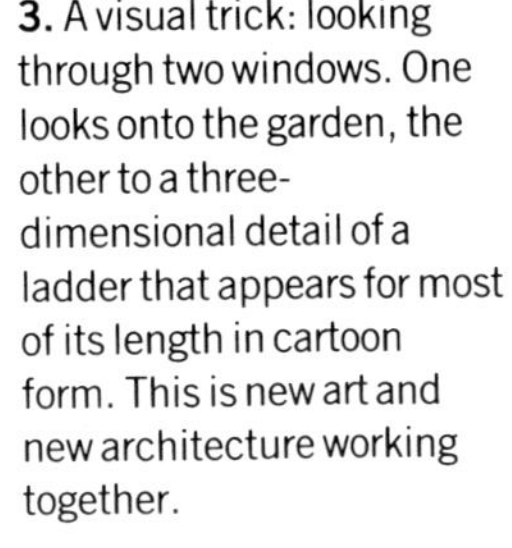

3. A visual trick: looking through two windows. One looks onto the garden, the other to a three-dimensional detail of a ladder that appears for most of its length in cartoon form. This is new art and new architecture working together.

1

2

WEBER APARTMENT
MUNICH, GERMANY
ANDREAS WEBER

1 & 2. By keeping this interior as clean and as clutter-free as possible, artworks are shown to effect.

3. New Modern interiors create links or visual bridges between domestic spaces: the eye is always led on, in this instance from the table, past the shelving and on through to the chair and sculpture in the room beyond.

3

1. In the bedroom, bed, rug, floor tiles, painting and window form a painterly composition of abstract planes. The painting might be the decorative high point of this room, yet the room is designed as an artwork in its own right, with each object contributing a major effect.

1

2

2 & 3. An engine-turned aluminum-topped table pays subtle homage to the industrial imagery that has often formed a part of 20th century design. Objects in contrasting metals placed on top of it make a romantic yet industrial still-life, accompanied here by ripe apples.

3

Traditional houses adapt well to New Modern interiors: old and new styles are complementary.

A place for history

1

SPIELBERG HOUSE
LONG ISLAND, USA
GWATHMEY SEIGEL

1. The crisp and clear-cut geometry of this house in the country betrays its recent origins. It might appear as old as its rural setting, but its regularity and clean construction prove otherwise. This is New Modernism in old garb.

2

2. The formal relationship between the house and its garden, as well as the overtly rational spacing of the windows, are all hints that New Modern concerns have brushed against the idea of this house. The balcony, glazed "lean-to" and skylight are further clues, as is the highly functional chimney which architect and client have chosen not to clad in fancy rural dress.

Modernists have long been accused of abandoning or denying history. This is not quite true. Certainly cultural extremists of the First World War era, such as the Italian Futurists, seemed to want to discard the cultural baggage of the past in favor of the machine and everything new. But these early histrionics gave way to an accommodation with history. Architects such as Le Corbusier and the Russian-born Berthold Lubetkin made their allegiance to the classical tradition quite clear. However, they were interested in the essence of classical rhythms and proportions and not in its formal expression. Even then, columns appeared in Corbusier's houses in the forms of undecorated *piloti*, while in the Highpoint Two apartment block in Highgate, London (1938–9), Lubetkin incorporated reproductions of the caryatids that hold up a cornice of the Erechtheion (421–405 BC) at the Acropolis, Athens, Greece. History was referred to or reinterpreted, but classical values were not abandoned by the more formal of the Modernists.

In this sense there is no discrepancy in living in a New Modern house in the 1990s and surrounding yourself with history. Nevertheless, in the free-flowing spaces and restrained surfaces of a New Modern interior history takes on a very different role than it does in a pseudo-historic home. In the latter there is a conscious attempt to recreate a vision of the past. You will be admitting, to varying degrees, that you would prefer to live in the past, or at least a sanitized version of the past, than in the present. There is nothing wrong with this. But New Modern living celebrates the attractions of the present while providing an elegant framework for the past.

In a grand 18th century Classical room sofas, occasional chairs, wall treatments, mirrors, plasterwork, carpets, paintings and other decorative objects were carefully considered as part of an artistic whole. The effect was univalent: it all went

3. Despite the old wooden struts and beams, this cool, white living room with its generous glimpses of spaces beyond, is very much in line with New Modern thinking. Note also the celebration of the stair and the geometric forms and patterns created by the central hearth. The house makes an optimum use of daylight. Windows are backed up with sophisticated modern climatic control: the ducts are on view.

1. The simple internal architecture acts as a sympathetic backdrop to equally simple period furniture. In a cluttered room both chair and tables seen here would be out of place or even hidden. Here they assume a major role in deciding the character of the room.

2. Buildings do not achieve a modernity of character solely through the use of modern materials. In this beautifully lit corner of the Spielberg house, traditional materials, furniture and decorative objects create a thoroughly modern and functional esthetic.

together. Early Modern architects and designers set out to do much the same, creating a comprehensive modern language of interior decoration. In this sense they were no different from the Neo-Classical, Gothic, Arts & Crafts and Art Nouveau architects and decorators of the 19th century. But for most people the strictures of a perfect Art Nouveau, De Stijl or Modern Movement house are simply too great. Furniture, paintings and objects from other periods appear out of place and irrelevant. They upset such insistent and finely tuned interiors. The problems of taking over and moving into such a house are huge. Are the new owners free to set their own character on the house, or are they custodians of a 20th century museum?

New Modern interiors offer a framework for

If the *chaise longue* was by Le Corbusier and the wall hanging by Eileen Gray; if the wrinkled timber pilaster were of bush-hammered concrete, this image would be pure Modern Movement. Instead, this grouping is a delightful juxtaposition of functional traditional and functional modern elements.

1

LEONARD APARTMENT
LONDON, ENGLAND
PETER LEONARD

1. Only the complex profile of the skirting board goes any way to dating this room in a London house of the 1850s. Otherwise this could easily be a room in a new city apartment. The crisp black sofa, the steel and glass tables and the neatly jointed floor reinforce the New Modern look.

2

2. Stripping a simple Victorian London developer's house to its basic shell, while retaining its decorative detailing and fixtures, often reveals a sequence of well-lit and well-proportioned rooms ideal for New Modern living.

history. Their spaces and decor can accomodate a Shaker chair, a Lacroix writing table, a William Burges washstand, a Jacques-Emile Ruhlmann card table as well as any piece by Charlotte Perriand, Charles Eames or Phillipe Starck, or something entirely new by Jaspar Morrison, Andre Dubreuil or Ron Arad. The setting for this New Modern eclecticism can either be a historic house decorated in a chaste manner such as Peter Leonard's Regency apartment in London, England, a white Modern interior such as Andreas Weber's apartment in Germany, (see page 116) or even a new barn designed to look old yet offering free-flowing living accommodation such as in the Spielberg house in America (see page 120).

The generous spaces that New Modern houses offer make it easier to accommodate historic furniture and art objects. A long-case clock, for example, will not fit comfortably or at all under the ceiling of a

2

2. In the 1950s and 1960s developers, politicians, planners and architects conspired to destroy rows of historic town houses because they failed to see the modern potential they offered. Rooms like these can accommodate both traditional and modern ways of living without need for major alteration.

new developers' house in Europe; but even the smallest New Modern houses, such as those designed by Pierre d'Avoine in Richmond, Surrey, England (see page 63), can take on board a tall clock, statue, painting or piece of furniture.

It is true that historic furniture, artworks and antiques take on a different role – and perhaps character – when placed in a New Modern interior. Out of historical context, without a complementary decorative backdrop, they can look like exhibits from a modern museum. But they can also be liberated in this way and seen to their best advantage.

Even so, historic furniture in New Modern homes looks best when adopted sparingly. It is the juxtaposition of a single piece of old and intricate furniture against the cool spaciousness of the New Modern interior that shows off both in the most favorable way. The less cluttered a modern room, the more impressive that single object becomes. Rather than culling antique markets for every item of marginally acceptable old furniture in an attempt to recreate some hazy historical vision, the New Modern passes these by, saving up for the one piece that really means something to them.

1. In modernizing old houses and apartments 20 and 30 years ago, many home owners ripped out period details in search of a clean, no-nonsense contemporary look. Fire surrounds fell particular prey to this denuding of old interiors. But, as this powerful marble surround proves, to be Modern does not have to mean a disrespect for history and precedent.

3. There are two main factors that distinguish this room in its New Modern guise from its original form. The first is the sparse but well-positioned pieces of furniture and the second the play of light. The modern polished floor reflects daylight as do the smooth, white plaster walls and silver objects. The simplicity of decor and arrangement is decidedly new age.

3

The New Modern kitchen is a glamorous machine. It is not a country parlor, but a celebration of modern machinery and utensils.

The functional kitchen

A modern kitchen is a small industrial workshop crammed with useful – as well as spurious – mechanical equipment and electronic wizardry. Stove, refrigerator, dishwasher, washer-dryer, microwave and a battery of subsidiary electric helpmates from toasters to blenders are all part of this domestic factory. Perhaps it was this surfeit of modern technology that encouraged the development of the pseudo-country fitted kitchen during the 1970s and 1980s. Without doubt, the most popular style for modern kitchens throughout the developed world remains a romanticized "country" look that serves to hide the mechanical, electronic and functional aspects of the kitchen.

But disguise goes against the New Modern grain. The New Modern kitchen is not ashamed of what it is. It resembles, for the most part, a ship's galley or a domestic engine room. Yet this machine for cooking in is not grim. Far from it. For example, the kitchen in the Rogers' house in London, England (see pages 22–3 and 133) is steely, shipshape and highly functional, yet it is also un-

1. Richard Sapper's chiming kettle for Alessi is one of a number of new, yet already familiar gadgets in modern kitchens.

WILD HOUSE
LONDON, ENGLAND
DAVID WILD

2. A kitchen that is a complex sequence of squares and rectangles. But this architectural rigor is suffused with light, softened by food and glasses and warmed by planes of color.

JOSEPH APARTMENT
LONDON, ENGLAND
EVA JIRICNA

3. The clean-cut, transparent quality of these kitchen shelves turns every object placed on them, from egg to *cafetiére*, into domestic sculpture.

4. The ship's galley, all tackle trim and stowed away, is quite clearly the inspiration behind this highly polished stainless steel kitchen.

Juno
Convectomat

1

NICK KNIGHT HOUSE
SURREY, ENGLAND
DAVID CHIPPERFIELD

1. An essay in industrial materials – steel, concrete and wood – all of which have become classic New Modern mediums. As well as their undoubted esthetic appeal, architects and designers choose them because they have the benefit of being practical, tough and long-lasting.

ROGERS HOUSE
LONDON, ENGLAND
RICHARD ROGERS

2. In a house where the owners are gourmets and the food they prepare is a visual as well as olefactory delight, it makes perfect sense to design a kitchen in plain view along the lines of an altar. It is impeccably functional.

doubtedly glamorous. This glamor is achieved by the use of high-quality surface finishes and by the kind of attention to detail you might expect in a quality automobile or helicopter. Architects like Richard Rogers and Eva Jiricna have proved that steel and aluminum surfaces and fittings are as attractive as anything that can be achieved with wood. Their kitchens have much the same appeal as the engine room of an ocean liner.

The New Modern kitchen is a special room with a character very much of its own. The stunning galley kitchen in the Gary Cunningham's converted Power Station, in Texas, USA (see page 134), is a fine example of how a kitchen can be distinctive, highly functional and yet the kind of living space that you are immediately drawn to.

There are, however, two very distinct schools of thought on how to deal with the increasingly complex gadgetry deemed essential in contemporary kitchens. In the extreme example of the Minimalist house in London designed by John Pawson and Claudio Silvestrin, the kitchen has been designed so that nothing at all is on display. Every piece of equipment is hidden behind a row of identical cupboard doors. While this kitchen appears to be as uncomplicated as that of a Cistercian monastery, it is in fact host to the usual array of electronic culinary helpmates.

In contrast, the kitchens found in the Texas Power House, or those of Richard Rogers and Eva Jiricna are, in part, celebrations of gadgetry, no matter how streamlined their fittings.

Whether a New Modern kitchen celebrates or tucks away gadgetry, fittings such as taps or faucets are always designed to be seen. As they are an essential and prominent part of any kitchen, they should be designed or chosen with as much care and attention as people spend when selecting a lamp, a bed or a chair.

Since the 1980s, designers have produced many new pieces of equipment specifically for self-consciously modern kitchens. Industrial designers such as Richard Sapper, well-known for his elegant, jointed Tizio reading lamp, produced a kettle that chimed like an American Amtrak express train. Since then, there have been a flood of entertaining new kitchen products; yet when it comes down to it, New Moderns prefer established classics to gimmickry and functional elegance to Post-Modern whimsy.

2

POWER STATION HOUSE
TEXAS, USA
GARY CUNNINGHAM

1. Another highly polished New Modern kitchen in the guise of a ship's galley. The translucent screen which forms the end wall ensures that this kitchen is separate, yet not disconnected from the rest of the house.

WYCHCOMBE STUDIOS,
LONDON, ENGLAND
RICK MATHER ARCHITECTS

2. Because Rick Mather has designed the kitchen as an integral part of the main living accommodation, it benefits from opening up into a bright double-height space.

4

SHINOHARA HOUSE
TOKYO, JAPAN
PROFESSOR SHINOHARA

3. The kitchen in this Japanese house is a natural outgrowth of the sloping walls, and appears to be one single unit or organism. Working surfaces are minimal, perhaps to accord with a taste for minimalist food.

MINIMALIST HOUSE
LONDON, ENGLAND
PAWSON AND SILVESTRIN

4 All equipment, from cutlery to dishwasher, is hidden away behind a run of identical cabinet doors, subverting the modern tendency to display gadgetry.

3

3

2

WEBER APARTMENT
MUNICH, GERMANY
ANDREAS WEBER

1. A corner of a kitchen that plays with Le Corbusier's dictum that the "house is a machine for living in." Steel and rubber materials and surfaces seem hard-edged, but are both functional and a part of a romantic dream about efficiency and technology.

2. Here, the kitchen is reduced to its most basic elements, but high-quality materials and equipment have been used to make sure that a minimalist style is not confused with meanness or lack of concern for texture. It is easy to keep a kitchen like this in perfect condition.

3. Simple New Modern rooms maximize daylight, which in turn concentrates attention on their essential qualities and aspects; here, there are flowers on the table, coffee ready on the worktop, glasses and dishes to hand.

4. The functional esthetic is taken to its logical limits with glass and ceramic ware that takes its cue from the laboratory rather than the cosy country kitchen. In this way, the simplest object seems somehow significant.

4

An elemental bathroom can be luxurious: minimal fittings are welcoming when well-made from warm-surfaced materials

The functional bathroom

The esthetic of the New Modern bathroom derives from several sources. The stainless steel bathrooms of Eva Jiricna take their cue from the compact and easily cleaned fittings of ocean-going yachts and airliners. The lavatories shoehorned into the tail section of modern airliners are a small triumph in terms of making maximum possible use of minimum space. In a tiny city apartment, this approach makes good sense. Much depends, however, on whether owners can make do with a compact shower room or demand the luxury of a large bathroom.

In the United States and in continental Europe many people are perfectly happy to install a shower rather than a bathtub, and if they have a tub, then they rarely use it. Both the British and the Japanese, however, still prefer to soak away the cares of the city in steaming baths. The height of luxury for many Britons, even New Moderns, is a very large white porcelain bathtub filled to the brim with hot

BJORNSEN HOUSE
LOS ANGELES, USA
ARATA ISOZAKI

1. While the prickly green cactus stores water in the dry Californian heat, the smooth chromed steel pool shower fitting ejects it at high speed.

GALLERY HOUSE
LONDON, ENGLAND
CHASSAY AND WILSON

2. Floor, basin and shower base are all sculpted from the same hard-wearing terrazzo.

OPEL HOUSE
VERMONT, USA
GWATHMEY SEIGEL

3. Like most New Modern bathrooms, the shower arrangement has been organized so that curtains or screens are unnecessary. The functional fitting aims one way only: down on the bather.

MINIMALIST HOUSE
LONDON, ENGLAND
PAWSON & SILVESTRIN

1 & 2. As bathrooms are designed to cleanse, it seems odd that they are so often cluttered. This chaste room is a celebration of cleanliness in spirit and letter (below). The adjacent lavatory is equally simple (right).

1

2

water; a place in which to read, sing and dream. The Japanese prefer their hot wooden tubs. These are often designed, like whirlpool baths, for several people to steam in at the same time.

New technology has meant that bathrooms, shower rooms and lavatories can be concealed in the smallest corner of a house, even in a space that lacks windows. However, this type of room can be intensely depressing. Despite the fact that technology can provide a complete bathroom in the tiniest space – as in the example of airliners – a bathroom with a view is still a highly desirable feature of any home, old or radically new.

Although imaginative design has increased the possibilities for using space for bathrooms, little effort has gone into the design of bathroom fittings, certainly nothing like the time and energy that designers and manufacturers have invested in new lamps and chairs. This may reflect the fact that people have not changed their pattern of washing and bathing very much over the centuries. In the 1960s several manufacturers commissioned ranges of ergonomic baths, sinks, bidets and toilets based on the latest research on the best way for people to perform bathroom activities. The results were a success from the point of view of ergonomics and health, but failed to woo buyers, who found the odd shapes uncomfortable to the eye. As a result, such ergonomic designs never reached the mass market, and they are as rare today as they were 25 years ago.

The ultimate New Modern bathroom is one in which the whole room is a machine for washing in. For example, the bathroom that John Pawson and Claudio Silvestrin designed for a London art dealer

3. Water and light are two purifying elements. Here, they are fused together to create a memorable corner of a custom-made New Modern bathroom. The washbasin has been designed to resemble a water stoup from a medieval Cistercian abbey – the most chaste and beautifully built of all European buildings. This allusion might seem arcane, but not to architect or client. The washbasin is carved from granite; its purity of form free from intrusive taps.

can be soaked – walls, floors, furniture, fittings and ceiling – with water. The minimal design and decoration of this bathroom means that there is nothing for water to spoil.

New technology can provide completely mechanized bathrooms. It is perfectly possible to design a bathroom that, hermetically sealed, can wash itself. The French street furniture manufacturer, Jean Claude-Decaux, has been installing automatic, self-cleansing public toilet facilities throughout western Europe over the past decade. The Sanisette automatic public convenience is a marvel of computer control, robotics and public health, yet many people are afraid to use them. The concept is brilliant, but even New Moderns have fixed ideas of what a bathroom should be like.

JOSEPH APARTMENT
LONDON, ENGLAND
EVA JIRICNA

1. The bathroom as a glamorous machine for washing in. There is unexpected warmth in the hard-edged fixtures and finishes.
2. A classic Modern mirror by architect Eileen Gray sets the theme for this New Modern bathroom. It is neatly offset by a stainless steel sink, drinking fountain and wall light.

LEONARD APARTMENT
LONDON, ENGLAND
PETER LEONARD

3. Here the designer has created a Modern feel, but softened the focus with Art Deco and traditional elements. Although essentially stark and simple, when lit the effect is one of New Modernism goes to Hollywood.

This is understandable given that for many people the bathtub or shower is the one place where they can relax completely and shut the rest of the world out. They do not want technology to intrude. Even a whispering electric air extractor can be upsetting when what is wanted is perfect calm. So while surfaces and textures might change, the New Modern bathroom remains very much the same room it was in ancient Roman or traditional Japanese houses.

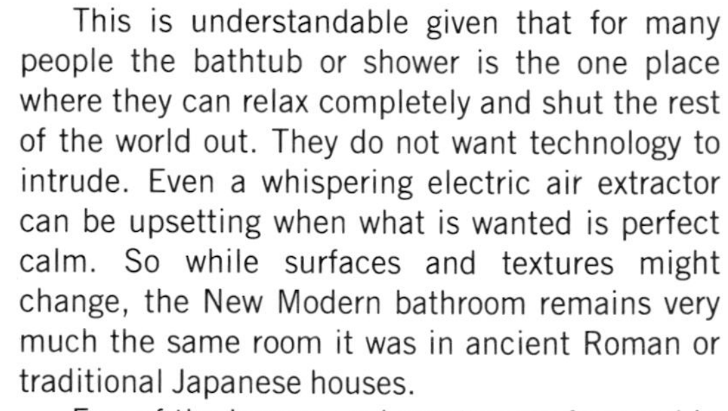

Few of the houses and apartments featured in this book show any signs of indulgent bathroom technology. Most are remarkably simple. New Moderns prefer fixed head showers to the omnidirectional variety which is so good at soaking floors. They prefer solid, simple bath and basin fittings to elaborate designs in gold finishes. The bathroom is not seen as a place to show off wealth and acquisitions, but as a space in which to relax.

This does not mean that a New Modern bathroom lacks drama or visual impact, nor that attention is not paid to every detail. The bathroom that Eva Jiricna has completed in her own London apartment (see page 145) is both glamorous and extremely functional. To achieve this, architects look beyond conventional suppliers to find the fittings they want. Increasingly the New Modern bathroom is custom-designed and custom-made.

4

BARNES APARTMENT
LONDON, ENGLAND
MUNKENBECK & MARSHALL

4. Industrial, medical and nautical fittings can all be adapted to create a New Modern look in bathrooms. But here the artist Danny Lane has been commissioned to make a beautifully simple sink entirely in glass, the sculptural taps reflected in the basin. The custom-made window gives views out while ensuring privacy.

2

JIRICNA APARTMENT
LONDON, ENGLAND
EVA JIRICNA

1. In this black, white and steely bathroom, Eva Jiricna has created an environment that is at once highly functional and romantic. It has all the qualities of the best Hollywood-style bathrooms of the 1930s and 1940s, yet its rigorous esthetic is derived from strictly European sources. The highly individual effect is achieved by a mixture of proprietary bathroom fittings and custom-made steel details.

2. A bathroom cabinet that proves just how romantic industrial materials can be, especially when mixed with mirrors and subtly diffused lighting.

3. There is no reason why bathrooms should be composed of conventional bathroom equipment designed for the domestic market when industrial fittings of this interest and quality are available.

4. Coexisting in this bright entrance lobby to a primarily dark bathroom is a mixture of nautical imagery and visual references to the early Modern houses of Le Corbusier.

3

4

1

1

SPIELBERG HOUSE
LONG ISLAND, USA
GWATHMEY SEIGEL

1. New Modern bathrooms are normally of two basic types: small, functional shower rooms for speedy ingress and exit and generous rooms designed for leisurely washing and pampering. They are not as utilitarian as might be thought – textures are warm and natural, they are well-lit, and additional interest is given by displays of folded, white towels.

2

3

GAREY HOUSE
CONNECTICUT, USA
GWATHMEY SEIGEL

2. Hemmed into tight spaces when land values are high, a bathroom does not need to feel claustrophobic. New Modern architects make a feature of internal windows to bring warm light to the smallest room.

OPEL HOUSE
VERMONT, USA
GWATHMEY SEIGEL

3. In this bathroom, the bath itself is built into a recess and made to appear as if it occupies a room beyond. This device heightens the spatial quality of the bathroom and obviates the need for a shower curtain.

1

POWER STATION HOUSE
TEXAS, USA
GARY CUNNINGHAM

1. Another example of a washbasin treated as a sculptural object. Custom-designed fittings like this do not need to be expensive. Metal washbowls inserted into sealed plywood stands can be less costly than proprietary ceramic stands and basins.

POWER STATION HOUSE
TEXAS, USA
GARY CUNNINGHAM

3. New Modern bathrooms draw their inspiration from a number of precedents: the ocean liner, the yacht, traditional Japanese bathrooms and Nordic saunas. The key is to keep the design uncluttered to reflect the idea of cleanliness.

2

MURPHY HOUSE
CALIFORNIA, USA
BRIAN MURPHY

2. The white-tiled bathroom is an expected feature of a modern house. Here, the tiles have been used to decorative effect, in keeping with an undercurrent of flamboyance that runs throughout the house.

3

4

5

4. Industrial fittings like this large basin have a solid generosity that many domestic fittings lack. White, marble and chrome lend an air of luxurious simplicity.

MURPHY HOUSE
CALIFORNIA, USA
BRIAN MURPHY

5. Glass bricks, a key motif of modern houses, can be used to real effect in bathrooms, where there is a demand for daylight and privacy. This is less important in shower rooms where speed takes priority over poetic light effects.

New Modern bedrooms are designed with the utmost simplicity. They are places for people to dream freely, away from the images imposed by everyday life.

The New Modern dream

2

MINIMALIST HOUSE
LONDON, ENGLAND
PAWSON & SILVESTRIN

1 & 2. Stripped to its essentials, this bedroom might seem a clinical place to rest. But free from domestic detritus, it is a place to escape the messiness of the working day in a city. The materials used are warm and natural (left). The childrens' rooms are placed in the converted attics. Wall-to-ceiling cupboards, virtually indistinguishable from the white walls, allow clothes and toys to be swept away tidily.

The bedroom has changed little in hundreds of years. It has rarely been more than a simple room with just enough space to accommodate a bed, dresser, washstand and some sort of chest or cupboard for storage. Only in 20th century Modern houses have architects, designers and their clients begun to explore the possibilities of bedroom design.

The main reason for change has been a simple question of space. As people squeeze into ever-smaller city apartments, the bedroom itself has become compact. A general rule in New Modern houses and apartments is that the living rooms should be as large as possible, while bedrooms can be shoehorned, if necessary, into the smallest possible space. Even so, this has not meant that

1

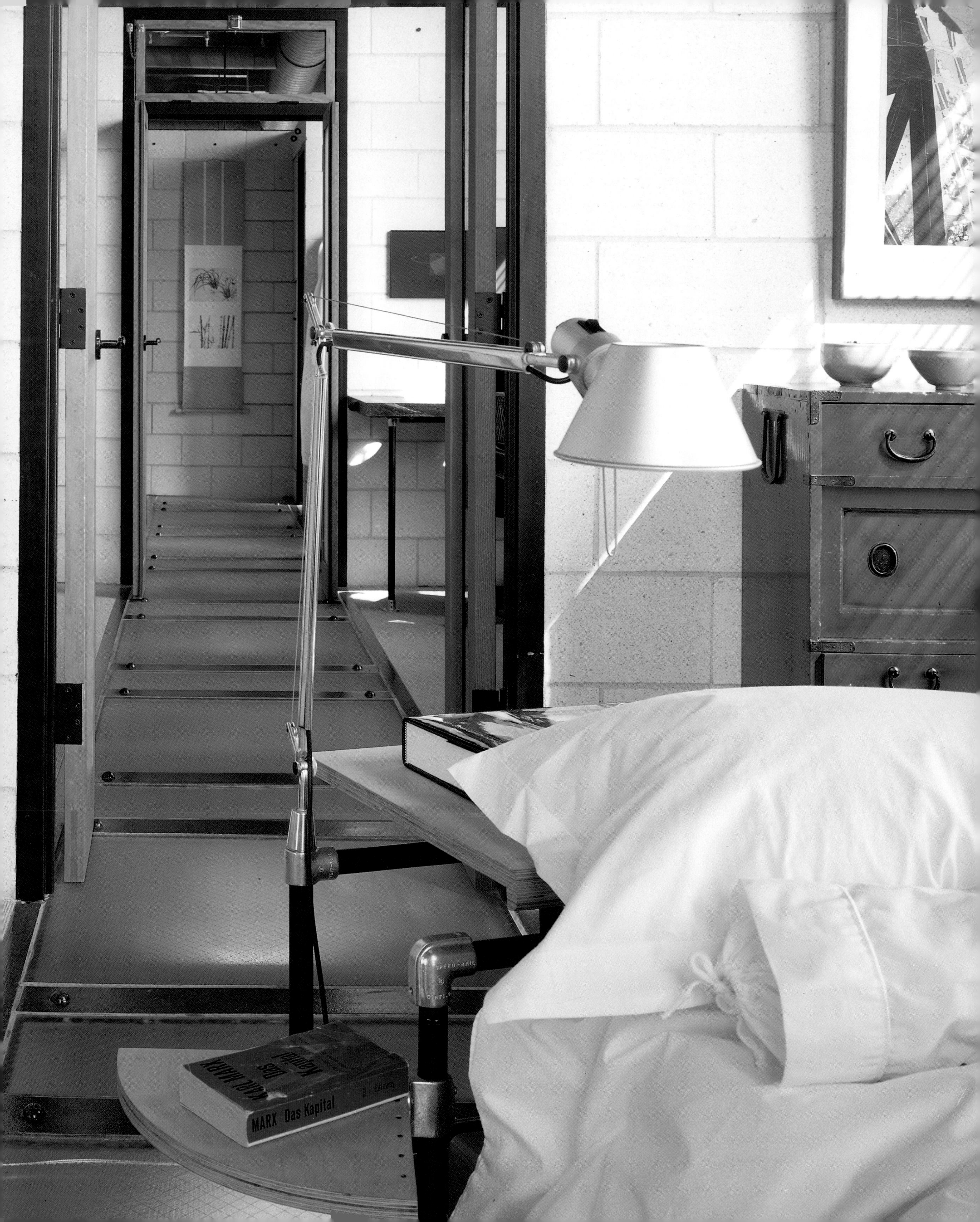
KARL MARX
Das Kapital
MARX Das Kapital

POWER STATION HOUSE
TEXAS, USA
GARY CUNNINGHAM

1. The esthetic here is seemingly drawn from the fictional world of Jules Vernes: this might be a bedroom in Captain Nemo's Nautilus. Note the glass floors lit from below and the engineered bedside lamp – the stuff of dreams.

the bedroom has become an insufferably small room; simply that its role has changed.

The temptation to cram in a conventional bed accompanied by the usual bedside cabinet and wardrobe is still a very strong one throughout the western world. The idea of a bedroom in which the bed takes up the whole space has only caught on in very recent years. Another latter-day innovation in the West is a Japanese-type bedroom in which mattress-style beds, known as futons, can be rolled up and stored away out of sleeping hours.

The first apartment that Eva Jiricna designed for fashion entrepreneur Joseph Ettedgui in London took the idea of the compact bedroom to its logical extreme. Partitioned between shelves that carried television, sound system and all the other accoutrements of rest, play and sleep, the bed itself filled the floorspace entirely. This arrangement meant that Joseph got the largest bed possible. He was able to shut himself off at night in a high-tech equivalent of a traditional four-poster.

2

3

BJORNSEN HOUSE
LOS ANGELES, USA
ARATA ISOZAKI

2. A secondary sleeping space is a small bunk reached by climbing up a stair from beside the dining room. Again, this offers paintings to look at rather than views out, although light pours in from the angled skylights.

3. Some dreams are more obvious than others. In keeping with the surreal artwork in this house, the bed rests on top of a large desk. Views out are into the real world (only by standing on tip toe), or into a fantasy canvas landscape.

Another space-saving solution is the sleeping loft. A dramatic early example was produced by the British architects James Stirling and James Gowan when they designed student dormitories in a late 1960s extension to Queen's College, Oxford, the Florey Building. Here, each student has an exceptionally tall, glazed living space. The bed is banished to a narrow loft at the top of a ladder-like stair, thus separating living, study and sleeping areas. Sleeping lofts make sense when there is space – for example underneath a roof – to create a small sleeping area, but not a decent-sized or serviceable room. Such a space can be made attractive largely by the design of an elegant or dramatic stairway to connect it to existing floors.

One of the mysteries of bedroom design has been the lack of views out, not when standing up, but when lying down. The pleasure of lying in bed while watching the world outside seems to be an entirely new one. David Chipperfield has designed just such a bedroom for fashion photographer Nick Knight (see page 155). Perhaps the fact that this arrangement means that the principal window has to be almost at floor level, rather than at the eye level of a person standing, disturbs conventional views of how a room and then facade of a building should be designed. To the New Modern, however, it is a practical and delightful solution.

NICK KNIGHT HOUSE
SURREY, ENGLAND
DAVID CHIPPERFIELD

1 & 2. In a New Modern house money otherwise spent on gratuitous decorative effects and objects can be invested in finely joined cupboards, designed to keep clutter at bay. These occupy one wall of the bedroom. The low-set window affords views of the garden to anyone resting in bed.

2

1

New Modern living opens up the tiniest house or apartment, creating a free flow of space where none seems to exist.

TWIN APARTMENTS
LONDON, ENGLAND
BIRDS PORTCHMOUTH & RUSSUM

These apartments are located on the roof of a Victorian town house, taking the place of the existing attic storey and thus creating space from what was a void.

1. Lightweight furniture set against a light, but plain backdrop helps to exaggerate the limited space available in this rooftop eyrie.

Living in small spaces

A miniature house or a house built to minimal space standards has no virtue to any normal person or family. Unless infirm or looking for a city *pied à terre* as a second home, most of us want as much space as we can get for our money. Given the limitation of available space in towns and cities it does seem odd that so many houses, particularly those built this century, should make such poor use of interior space. Poorly arranged rooms that connect awkwardly with one another, ill-lit lobbies, stairs, landings and corridors, wasted loftspace: all these are characteristics of the typical 20th century family house, whether in Chicago, London or Frankfurt.

Early Modern Movement architects, notably Walter Gropius and Mies van der Rohe working in Germany in the 1920s, sincerely believed that minimizing domestic space was a virtue. They designed and built apartment houses for German workers with what most of us would consider impossibly low ceilings, tiny galley-like kitchens and narrow corridors. What was known as *Existenzminimum* housing was intended to prove that families in cities needed only a minimum of space in which to eat, sleep and wash. *Existenzminimum* apartments would be easy to clean, cheap to heat and preserve as much green space as possible in inner city areas.

Although logical, this way of thinking was too scientific, altogether too cold, logical, rigorous and ultimately mean for normal human beings. While a high ceiling might make a house or apartment more expensive to heat, and while it might be difficult to clean, it allows people to breathe and to dream more freely. High ceilings impart a sense of grandeur and well-being. Modern Movement architects made themselves unpopular by insisting on describing any space in a building that seemed superfluous to functional requirements as "redundant" space. But it is just that redundant space – a high ceiling, a grand stair, an airy lobby – that makes a house delightful.

New Modern architects see space very differently from their austere predecessors. Their aim is to extract the maximum possible living space from any set of measurements, whether a small city apartment or a detached suburban house. They believe in *existenzmaximum*, knowing that what most people want in their homes above all is space,

3

4

2. A conventional ceiling could have divided this double-height space. This would have given more useable floor area, yet it would also have made the apartment seem much meaner than it actually appears.

3. Scaled-down fittings allow a small, open-plan kitchen to be well-serviced.

4. An adequate radiator can dominate a small bathroom. Here, Russem has chosen to make a sculptural virtue of a domestic necessity.

TURIN APARTMENTS
TURIN, ITALY
CAVAGLIA

1. Roof spaces are no restriction to New Moderns. The keys to extending limited space are scale, materials and light. Note the proportions of the door, the extended rooflights, polished terrazzo floor and lightweight furniture.

2

2, 3 & 4. Access to even the smallest garden alleviates the potential problem of limited interior space (left). Televisions do not need to gobble up space (below). Small interiors make the most use of space when details and decoration are scaled down to suit. Here screens, door handles and door frames are all reduced to an elegant minimum (bottom).

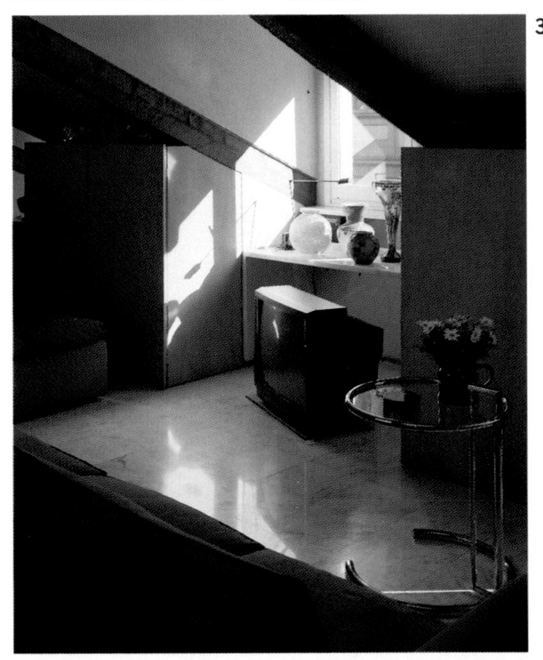

3

1

light and freedom of movement. New Modern design has the immediate advantage of offering the maximum possible useable space inside four walls. By abandoning conventional house plans and considering each house afresh, architects can work with their clients to create generous living spaces in even the smallest house.

The art of maximizing minimal space is one practised on several levels. For example, in an existing house or apartment, rooms can be rearranged. Walls that are really no more than partitions can easily be dispensed with. Even loadbearing walls can be removed as long as the architect knows how to transfer the weight of the house safely onto remaining walls. Ceilings can disappear too. In fact, a house can easily be shorn to virtually a bare shell and its interior rebuilt, so that it becomes an essay in light and freedom of movement rather than a dull story of box-like rooms, dark, inconvenient and wasted spaces. However, such dramatic treatment to a house is unjustified if the interior is of historic value. Better to look for a drab, ordinary 20th century house that can be gutted and remodelled, rather than ripping out an interior that you might not like personally, but which is of historic importance.

New houses in suburban areas where land prices are high can also be designed with an enhanced sense of space. Too often, housebuilders assume that the average family wants a very average house. If detached, this will normally comprise two reception rooms, a kitchen, two large bedrooms, a boxroom and a bathroom. The New Modern house offers flexibility. The row of small houses designed by the London architect Pierre d'Avoine in Surrey, England (see page 63) are a perfect illustration of just how different and spacious a small two-bedroom townhouse can be.

And the New Moderns have other tricks up their sleeves. Space can also be stretched by the use of color, mirrors and glass, by the use of moveable or sliding partitions rather than solid walls, by the opening up of double-height spaces, by the design of lightweight stairs and through the use of finishes that reflect light rather than absorbing it.

One of the characteristics of New Modern thinking is its willingness to absorb design ideas

4

1

TURIN APARTMENTS
TURIN, ITALY
CAVAGLIA

1. This simple modern bathroom makes full use of limited ceiling height. Although tucked into the eaves, the design and decor ensures that the room is light and airy.

2

3

from other cultures. Japanese architects, for example, have long studied and practised the art of extracting maximum space from minimal surroundings. The serenity of the Japanese interior, with its use of natural materials and translucent sliding screens, also depends on its minimal use of furniture. Modern European or American interiors can be offputting to many people, given their use of steely furniture and fittings. The Japanese interior shows how natural materials can be used to evoke a world of fine craftmanship in what can be tiny city apartments. A miniature house today no longer need be a machine for living in, but an object of beauty and contemplation as well as a practical home for a small family.

2. Wherever possible, New Modern houses offer access to the outside world, even if a door leads only to the tiniest terrace or balcony. Shutters are an interesting alternative to curtains because they allow slants of daylight to filter through on hot days.

4

5

3 & 5. The small cloakroom (far left) has a purpose-made sink. The kitchen (above) makes use of a number of familiar materials and fittings, yet although conventional in this way, its freshness emerges in the complete lack of clutter. Storage is designed to maintain this domestic order.
4. In small interiors, glass partitions can be used to separate small rooms. They ensure that a room, such as the one seen here, is not cut off from daylight. At night, these partitions become a tantalizing wall of warm electric light.

1

2

4

HIGH-TECH HOUSE
LONDON, ENGLAND
NICHOLAS GRIMSHAW

1. A double-height living room might seem a luxury in a compact town house, but New Modern home owners are willing to trade some space for the luxury of light. The bedroom window gives onto views both outside and into the atrium.

2 & 3. The variety in the treatment of windows in this house – part of a new London terrace – enriches both the stainless steel facades and the character of the interiors (left). A porthole looks into the bright, compact kitchen-diner (below).

4. The main window fronting the kitchen-diner can be raised on warm days. An electric motor lifts the hinged structure in much the same way as the roof of a convertible. Small town houses can get stuffy and seem confining on hot days; the New Modern approach used here has ensured that the owners benefit from the best of London weather.

3

1

2

BRINKERS APARTMENT
LONDON, ENGLAND
RON BRINKERS

1 & 2. A generous, curved sweep gives complete individuality to this living room. It is hard to believe that it is set in an apartment converted from the top floor of an ordinary late 19th century family house.

2

1 & 3. Although often chosen for its sculptural value, the spiral stair is not merely decorative. It has an important function as an ingenious spacing-saving device.

2. Here the disadvantages of the awkward angles found in converted attic spaces have been turned into an advantage by exploiting its geometry. Note how the stair rail echoes the roof lines.

3

GALLERY HOUSE
LONDON, ENGLAND
CHASSAY AND WILSON

1. To evoke a sense of space, the design and decoration of a small room needs to be based on one simple idea carried through with a gentle, yet relentless logic. Even then, there is scope for sculptural elements such as the baffle seen hanging over the desk.
2. Bringing daylight into a small space is not a problem if the designer thinks in terms of taking windows, no matter how narrow, from floor to ceiling, rather than cutting them off at waist height. The plain, polished surfaces of floor and walls, boosted by electric light, reflect light filtering through this lancet.

1

The New Modern house is at home in the country as it is in town. Its generous views out brings it close to nature. Houses need no longer be folksy when faced with the great outdoors.

Inside meets outside

There is no one prescribed form of New Modern garden. Some modern houses stand in old grounds, some in romantic new landscapes, yet others give onto Japanese gardens. Even then, some of these are made of hard, ungiving concrete, while others abound with ponds and oriental blossom. The most important aspect of the New Modern garden is not its plan or its smells or colors, but its relationship with the new architecture. New Modern houses are often designed to connect very closely with their surroundings, not in an organic way as, for example, with houses of the Arts & Crafts movement, but in apposition. So the starkest New Modern house will offer generous views of surrounding gardens. Often, windows are designed to give optimum views. Sometimes these are of a cinematic quality – as for example with the Opel House in Vermont, USA by Gwathmey Siegel – and sometimes of a deliberately restricted nature, as with the London house designed by John Pawson and Claudio Silvestrin, where the green of the garden is revealed only in segments.

In other houses, especially those in Japan or of Japanese derivation, the views from inside often give onto enclosed and very formal gardens. These are designed for quiet contemplation; they offer a buffer zone between the ordered man-made world and the planned chaos of nature. This type of Japanese garden is normally seen as extra living quarters, an outside room, and is therefore defined by walls. In the case of the house designed by David Chipperfield in Surrey, England (see page 32), the garden is intimately connected to the house – as far as possible it has been made a part of the uncompromising architecture.

It is possible to design a chaste or austere garden that accords with the esthetic of the severest New Modern house. Again, in the examples of the Pawson-Silvestrin and the Chipperfield houses, this possibility is powerfully realized. The garden John Pawson and Claudio Silvestrin have designed is as minimal as the architecture and decoration of the house. It is nothing more than a perfect geometrical, emerald-green lawn surrounded by high brick walls. House and garden share the same ideal. Both also make quite stringent demands on their owners. To maintain this ordered esthetic, the lawn must be kept free from intruding weeds, exactly as the walls of the house must be repainted at intervals to keep them as white as virgin snow.

2

3

GAREY HOUSE
CONNECTICUT, USA
GWATHMEY SIEGEL

1. Landscape paintings are hardly necessary when nature becomes a permanent and ever-changing backdrop to the main living space of a New Modern house. Decoration need only be minimal when an interior is set against nature.
2. The organic, yet ordered lines of this powerfully sculpted house act as a foil to natural growth. House and countryside complement one another.
3. Architecture and nature are mutually enhanced when set in thoughtful contrast. Shadows of trees fall across white walls and four-square windows, while the trees themselves look more luxuriant for being set against this particular backdrop.

1

WACHTER VILLA
ANTWERP, BELGIUM
JO CREPAIN

1. Early Modern Movement architecture was often in contrast to nature. New Modern houses are more accommodating, as can be seen from the plants entwining themselves around these breezeblock entrance pylons.
2. The building materials used in the construction of this house could hardly be less giving. Yet the siting of the house and its courtyard seem to embrace their natural surroundings. Although decidedly Modern, the columns echo the ancient notion that the classical column was adapted from contemplation of the tree trunk.

The idea of nature and the machine-esthetic working closely together might seem contradictory. Yet this is something that the best Modern Movement architects were always concerned with. When Le Corbusier designed his ideal cities in the 1920s, he planned to raise his buildings on *piloti* (concrete stilts). This would allow nature to cut a green swathe right through the heart of industrial cities: the buildings would stand above landscaped urban parkland to which everybody would have access. In this sense, the social thinking behind machine-age architecture was considerably more generous than any before it. The sad thing is that when European cities were rebuilt in the 1940s, 1950s and 1960s, the new architecture appeared without the swathes of green. The counterpoise Le Corbusier dreamed of could only be achieved with houses built for affluent private clients.

In the garden of the Chipperfield-designed house, trees are planted on a geometric grid. Eventually they will mature to provide an exterior room lined with neat rows of natural columns. This idea is more romantic than that seen in contemporary architect-designed gardens in Japan. The garden designed by Tadao Ando (see page 64) is a celebration of the concrete-maker's skill rather than a homage to nature. It works on a different premise from western gardens. Part of the idea is that a single plant contains within it the whole natural world. In contrast, most New Modern houses in America are designed like ships in a sea of plant life. In the work of such architects as Richard Meier, the house is a pristine white ocean-liner from which the landscape is observed like the furrows of the ocean.

The New Modern tradition has also come to terms with wood, again, most notably in the United States, where some of the most impressive out-of-town houses are built using traditional methods to achieve new architectural goals. The Opel house by Gwathmey Siegel is built in warm wood that connects closely with nature, yet is never anything less than overtly Modern.

3. Looking from the inside outward, the house moves in steady progression from an almost industrial esthetic – reflected in the building materials and the complex grids of the glass, brick and steel roof – to a meeting with its lush green surroundings.
4. In summer delicate drapes are hung from curtain poles that run across the columned front of the garden courtyard. Seen billowing through the naturally decorated columns, these drapes perform a remarkable job in blurring the edges between the severe forms of the house and its romantic setting.

2

OPEL HOUSE
VERMONT, USA
GWATHMEY SIEGEL

1. Sunlight on water and on walls, on glass and on steel, works in a striking, yet entirely natural fashion to forge a link between the graphic lines of this house and its garden. During the day, light reflecting off the swimming pool – dug in closely to the walls of the house – peppers the building with animated shadows. New Modern houses gain decorative effect from the simplest means.

KIDOSAKI HOUSE
TOKYO, JAPAN
TADAO ANDO

2. In this house nature is enclosed for contemplation within the architectural boundary. The courtyard is both a formal garden and an external room. Trees are carefully related to pot and steps.

3. Although a private and enclosed space, the garden is open, if only just, to the world beyond; the slits in the concrete walls are like windows. The hard concrete is a pleasurable contrast with the living trees.

3

1

GLENORIE HOUSE
SYDNEY, AUSTRALIA
GLEN MURCUTT

1. This corrugated steel and timber house has a very particular relationship with nature. It is raised on stilts to keep exotic insects and snakes at bay, as well as to help cool the interior in blisteringly hot summers. This is a traditional form brought up to date.
2. The deep verandah and its corrugated roof keep the sun at bay, while tall trees provide further protection.
3. Glen Murcutt calls this 'the meditation verandah.' Here man, safe in his crisp, industrial house is confronted face-to-face with raw nature.

3

2

Furniture and fittings

2

New Modern houses do not prohibit antique or traditional furniture. Because the shell of a new house is stripped to essentials, or otherwise makes no concessions to history, there is no need to dismiss family heirlooms. The architecture of a New Modern house is such that it acts as a frame for furniture, art and decorative objects of other periods. However, it is true that old furniture and paintings can never blend into a New Modern interior. Instead, they are framed by the architecture. They stand out in relief and, as a result, are often more noticed and all the more closely studied than those crammed into a conventional pseudo-classical or genuine historic interior.

However, in some extreme cases, traditional furniture is undesirable or else would look out of place. In the houses designed by David Chipperfield and by John Pawson and Claudio Silvestrin in London, the aim of both architect and client has been not just to escape from traditional furniture, but to reduce the amount of furniture to a minimum. Claudio Silvestrin would have preferred his clients to manage with nothing other than the fixed furniture, chairs, tables and worktops that are part of the architectural fabric of the house. In a new house in Majorca, Silvestrin has achieved precisely this effect. Nevertheless, this particular New Modern house is a holiday home, not a house for daily occupation by a family. This desire to do away with conventional furniture is rooted in the architecture of Cistercian abbeys, in traditional Japanese houses and in the writings and houses of Adolf Loos, the Viennese architect who believed that ornament was crime.

A strict attitude toward the use of furniture is also evident in another school of design. In houses that can be loosely gathered together under the label "High-tech," antique furniture looks completely out of place. Instead, pieces designed to echo the shapes and forms of airships, aircraft, yachts and cars are appropriate. Such furniture is freely available. Some of the best High-tech designs date back to the 1930s. Hans Coray's lightweight aluminum armchair, for example, is a favourite among High-tech architects and designers. Designed in 1930 for use in airship lounges, its lightweight structure and purity of form suggest that it might have been conceived much later.

Where cost allows, High-tech designers will use fittings designed for the aviation or automobile

1

KIDOSAKI HOUSE
TOKYO, JAPAN
TADAO ANDO

1. New Modern Japanese or Japanese-influenced interiors contain very little furniture. Where used, it acts as formal sculpture as well as conventional furniture. Here, Ando adds his own designs to simple, if dramatic effect.

BARNES APARTMENT
LONDON, ENGLAND
MUNKENBECK & MARSHALL

2. Simple, custom-made metal and glass shelves create sharply focused and distinctive lines in a London apartment. Making one-off pieces need not incur any more expense than buying ready-made shelves from a store.

1

NICK KNIGHT HOUSE
SURREY, ENGLAND
DAVID CHIPPERFIELD

1. A welded steel chair by Andre Dubreuil animates this studio; the hard, but flowing form of the chair is highlighted by the architecture.

SHINOHARA HOUSE
TOKYO, JAPAN
PROFESSOR SHINOHARA

2. These chairs and table are custom-designed to follow the geometry of the kitchen-diner and the triangular shape of its windows.

BRINKERS APARTMENT
LONDON, ENGLAND
RON BRINKERS

3. A mix of mathematics and the organic in this dining chair by D'Soto complements the crisp planes of the room. New Modern furniture often combines natural forms with geometry.

industries. However, these are often expensive. A chair that proved popular throughout Europe, Japan and the United States during the 1980s – and which is still selling strongly – is Ron Arad's Rover Chair. Arad bought a stock of leather seats from abandoned or scrapped Rover 2000 cars, mounting them on curved, matte black tubular steel frames. This homage to the automobile provided a reclining leather chair appropriate to the technologically inspired interiors.

The nice irony is that automobile seats are normally far more comfortable than most traditional chairs, many of which were designed for display rather than for sitting in for any length of time. Richard Rogers, architect of the Pompidou Center in Paris and the Lloyd's headquarters in the City of London, gives his Rover Chair pride of place in his minimalist, machine-esthetic house in London's Chelsea. "It makes me smile to see it," says Rogers, "but it also says a lot about materials and design. And pieces like this prove that in Arad we have a poet of technology."

Like Ron Arad, architects such as Eva Jiricna have shown that proprietary industrial parts bought from factory warehouses can be transformed into convincing, convenient and even comfortable modern furniture. Both Jiricna and Arad have been keen exponents of "Kee Klamp," a relatively inexpensive construction system designed principally for shelving and often used in exhibition stands. However, such is the flexibility and such are the possibilities of the "Kee Klamp" system that it is possible to design chairs, sofas and beds from it. Although Jiricna and Arad's work was in harmony in the early 1980s, they have since developed in different directions. Eva Jiricna has continued to refine her technologically inspired approach to architecture, interior design and furniture, while Arad has moved further into the realm of abstract experiments in metal.

New Moderns have their own equivalent of the traditionalist's Chippendale or Sheraton furniture. In very many modern interiors it is possible to use Modern Movement classics such as steel and chrome chairs by Marcel Breuer, Charlotte Perriand and Le Corbusier, and Charles and Ray Eames. And the past few years has seen a new avant-garde furniture slowly but surely making its way into New Modern homes. This ranges from the classic Modern Movement purity of Jasper Morrison's work to the often flamboyant metal artistry of Ron Arad.

Both classic Modern and New Modern furniture design have a strong connection with certain earlier forms. Shaker furniture, for example, along with other stripped-to-the-bone historic furniture, is very close in form and character to much Modern Movement design. This should not be surprising, as the aims were much the same. The Shakers made furniture that was simple, practical and true to the materials in which it was crafted. As a result, when placed alongside its contemporaries, Shaker furniture appears disconcertingly modern.

2

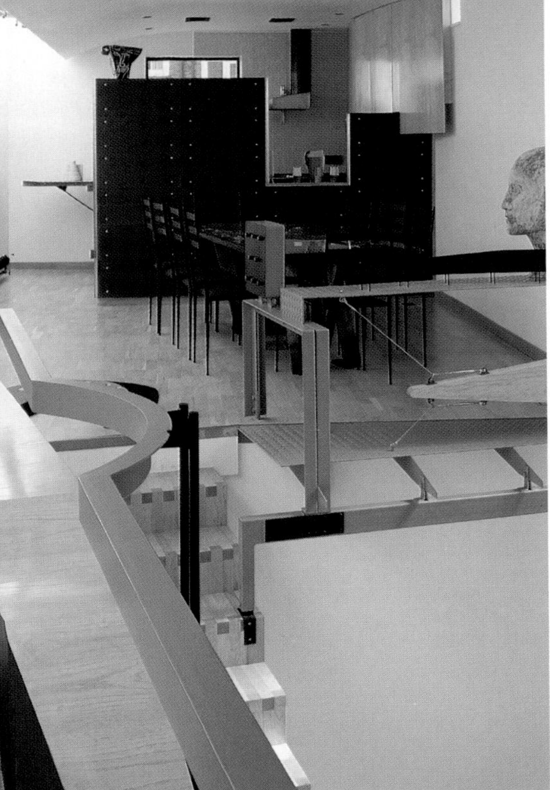

2

GALLERY HOUSE
LONDON, ENGLAND
CHASSAY AND WILSON

1. Each component of this house has been made to stand out. Even the light switches have been specially housed in a black box at the top of the stairs. Functional details have not been left to chance, so that the concept of the house as an artwork is not lost.

3

2. Every detail of this house has been specially made. The house is a gallery for showing new artworks. Furniture has either been custom-designed for the building or is shown for sculptural effect. And each fitting stands up as a small artwork.

3. This section of stair shows the level to which attention to detail has been taken by the architect. Even the umbrella stand has a style and character of its own. Throughout the house metal furniture and fittings contrast with those made of solid wood.

New Modern home-owners, unlike owners of the earlier uncompromising Modern Movement houses, are able to enjoy a variety of furniture – historic, traditional, Modern and avant-garde – without feeling compromised. The secret is to choose only the best furniture from any period.

New Modern houses have also developed their own vocabulary in detailed fittings. Some of these can be found in many of the houses illustrated in this book. The use of fine steel cable stretched taut up stairways and across mezzanine railings is common. So, too, are polished wooden floors and banister rails. These details have been developed and refined in a large number of houses and have now become classic features of New Modern house design.

Another such feature is the ubiquitous Venetian blind. Metal blinds, with finer slats than the type used by the original Modern Movement architects, are very much part of New Modern design. Blinds replaced curtains for a number of reasons. They have a satisfying mechanical quality; they filter light on bright days, casting abstract shadows on sealed and polished wooden floors; and although they attract dust, they are easy to clean. However, despite the blind's esthetic and functional advantages, curtains have become popular again in the 1990s. Full-length white curtains blowing in the breeze add texture and romance to an otherwise hard-edged New Modern interior (see page 173).

1

2

LYMAN APARTMENT
LONDON, ENGLAND
STEVE LYMAN

1. Basic modern materials can be used to original effect. Here, off-the-shelf materials and components have been used to create a corner cupboard. It has a character of its own, yet it fulfils the New Modern brief, which is to use materials simply.

2 & 3. Modern materials and Modern forms can work together with a basic traditional interior. There are no fittings or pieces of furniture in this room that are distinctly Modern, yet the effect *is* distinctly Modern, created by simple lines and colours.

4. A geometrical treatment has been given to this corner cabinet, which makes references to De Stijl design. It is an attempt to make imaginative use of the space between two chimney breasts. In small houses storage is at a premium, but it can be made an imaginative feature rather than a blank intrusion.

3

4

3

2

CUBIST APARTMENT
NEW YORK, USA
STEVEN HOLL

1 & 2. Chairs, table, cupboards and light fittings have been either designed or bought in to create a single esthetic, one that runs convincingly through this city apartment.
In small or modest-sized city apartments a simple color scheme carried right through creates a greater sense of space – and cohesion – than a fussy mix and match of color and decorative schemes.

SHINOHARA HOUSE
TOKYO, JAPAN
PROFESSOR SHINOHARA

3 & 4. The contrast between this interior and that of the Cubist apartment in New York (shown opposite) could hardly be greater, yet they have in common a visual consistency — no matter how bizarre — that runs from architecture to color through to furniture and fittings. All the furniture in this house was custom-designed for it by the architect-owner.

4

STORES

The shops, suppliers and galleries listed in this section specialize in contemporary furniture, lighting, textiles and decorative objects.

LONDON

Aram Designs
3 Kean Street
WC2
(071) 240 3933

Artemide
17-19 Neal Street
WC2
(071) 240 2552

Authentics
42 Shelton Street
WC2
(071) 240 9845

The Conran Shop
Michelin House
81 Fulham Road
SW3 6RD
(071) 589 7401

Coexistence
Hobhouse Court
18 Whitcomb Street
WC2
(071) 839 6353

Contemporary Textile Gallery
10 Golden Square
W1
(071) 439 9070

Crucial
204 Kensington Park Road
W11
(071) 229 1940

David Davies
10-11 Great Newport Street
WC2
(071) 240 2223

Diametrics
18 Odhams Walk
Long Acre
WC2
(071) 833 2838

Erco Lighting
38 Dover Street
W1
(071) 408 0320

Environment
15 Rosemont Road
NW3
(071) 435 3827

Freuds
198 Shaftesbury Avenue
WC2
(071) 831 1071

Heal & Son
196 Tottenham Court Road
W1
(071) 636 1666

Ikon
Metropolitan Wharf
Wapping Wall
E1
(071) 702 4828

Liberty
Regent Street
W1
(071) 734 1234

London Lighting
135 Fulham Road
SW3
(071) 589 3612

Maison
917 Fulham Road
SW6
(071) 736 3121

Marcatré
179–199 Shaftesbury Avenue
WC2
(071) 739 6865

Mary Fox Linton
249 Fulham Road
SW3
(071) 351 0273

Oggetti
133 Fulham Road
SW3
(071) 581 8088
& 101 Jermyn Street
W1
(071) 930 4694

One Off
62 Chalk Farm Road
NW1
(071) 379 0499

OMK
Stephen Building
Stephen Street
W1
(071) 631 1335

Oscar Woolens
81–85 Hampstead Road
NW1
(071) 387 5840

Rosenthal Studio House
120 Brompton Road
SW3
(071) 584 0683

SCP
135–139 Curtain Road
EC2
(071) 739 1869

SKK Lighting
110 Gloucester Avenue
NW1
(071) 488 2677

Viaduct
Spring House
10 Spring Place
NW5
(071) 284 0156

Vitra
13 Grosvenor Street
W1
(071) 408 1122

Wilson & Gough
106 Draycott Avenue
SW3
(071) 823 7082

MILAN

Alchimia
Museo Alchimia
via Torino 68

Alias
via Resphigi 2
20122

Arketipo
via Garibaldi 72
(Calenzano)

Arredaesse
via Montenapoleone 26

Artemide
via della Brughiera
20010

B & B Italia
corso Vittorio Emmanuele

Design Gallery Milano
via Manzoni 46

Driade
via Brera 16

Flos
corso Monforte 9

Italhome
via Palermo 1

PARIS

AvantScène
4 place de l'Odéon
75006
46 33 12 40

Axis
18 rue Guenegaud
75006
43 29 96 23

Cheska Vallois
33 rue du Seiné

Diffusion Bernard Carant
41 boulevard des Bastignolles
75008
45 22 43 14

Edifice
27 bis, boulevard Raspai
#75007
45 48 53 60

En Attendant les Barbares
50 rue Etienne Marcel
42 33 37 87

Etat de Siège
17 rue Lammenais
75008
42 29 31 60

Jean-Michel Wilmotte
5 place de l'Odéon
75006

Lieux
5 rue Ste Croix de la Bretonnerie
75003
42 33 37 87

Manuel Canovas
5 rue de Furstenberg

Protis
153 rue du Foubourg Saint Honore
75008
45 62 22 40

Via
10 place Ste Opportune
75001
42 33 14 33

Zumsteg
4 rue de Furstenberg

BARCELONA

Atri
Balmes 427

B.D. Ediciones de Diseno
Mallorca 91

Cisneros
Balmes 172

Diseno y Promocion
Bonavista 3

Mobisa
Cea Bermudez 56

Mobidal
San Antonio. M. Claret 103

Mobles 114
Enric Granados 114

Norman & Sicart
Muntaner 292

Pilma
Diagonal 403
& Llansa 33

Riera
Paseo de Gracia 91

Vincou
Paseo de Gracia 96

Xavier Pujol
Arago 332

TOKYO

Attic Trading Inc
298 Higashi
Shibuya-Ku

Casatec Ltd
296 Higashi
Shibuya-Ku

Eishin Trading Co Ltd
65 Morishita Chome 3
Koto-Ku

Eternal
3F Nakajima
31715
Nishiazabu
Minatoku

Gendai Kikakushitsu
Koshin Bldg
302 225
Sarugakucho
Chiyoda-Ku

Hiroshi Awatsuji Design Studio
1211
Jingumae
Shibuya-Ku

Idee
5444 Minamiaoyama
Minato-Ku

Itoki Co Ltd
151 Shibuya
2Chome
Shibuya-Ku

Kiya Gallery
92 SarugakuCho
Shibuya-Ku

Royal Furniture Collection
Coop Broadway Center
Room 1003
55215 Ivakano-Ku

Italia Shoji Co Ltd
54 Kojimachi
1 Chome
Chiyoda-Ku

Itoki Co Ltd
151 Shibuya 2 Chome
Shibuya-Ku

Nova Oshima Co Ltd
Kakakura Building
Akasaka Minato-Ku

Tanifuji Co Ltd
167
ShinyokohamaCho
Kohoku-Ku
KanagawaKen 222

NEW YORK

Furniture of the
Twentieth Century
227 West 17th Street
NY 10011

Luten Clarey Stern
1059 3rd Avenue
NY 10021

SEE Ltd
920 Broadway
NY 10020

Palazetti
515 Madison Avenue
NY 10022

Hammacher
Schlemmer
147 East 57th Street
NY 10022

George Kovacs
330 East 59th Street
NY 10022

Modern Age
795 Broadway
NY 10003

Stendig International
305 East 63rd Street
NY 10021

International Contract
Furnishing
305 East 63rd Street
NY 10021

International Design
Center
2030 Thompson
Avenue
Long Island City
NY 11101

Gallery 91
91 Grand Street
NY 10013

Dakota Jackson Inc
306 East 61st Street
NY 10021

Koch & Lowy
2124 39th Avenue
Long Island City
NY 11101

Modern Age Galleries
795 Broadway
NY 10003

Melodrom Ltd
525 Broadway
NY 10012

WEST GERMANY

Abitare
35 Auf dem Berlich
5000 Köln 1

Agentur Brunnbauer
Ehmcekstrasse 51
2800 Bremen 33

Andreas Weber
Nymphenburgerstrasse
79
8000 München 19

Bernd Schmidt
25 Tannenweg
8000 München 50

Design M Ingo Maurer
Kaiserstrasse 47
8000 München 40

DTec Industriedesign
Telleringstrasse
4000 Düsseldorf

Designwerkstatt Berlin
Yorckstrasse 88d
1000 Berlin 61

Elvira Handwerker
Muhlonstrasse 810
7766 Gaienhofer

Marianne Bruchhauser
Stautstrasse 13
2900 Oldenburg

Naefke & Co
Eppendorfer
Landstrasse 60
2000 Hamburg 20

Peter Pfeifer Focus
87 Leopoldstrasse
40 München 8

Traudel Comte
1 Alfred-Drexlstrasse
8000 München 50

ARCHITECTS

Tadao Ando Architect &
Associates
5–23 Toyosaki 2
Chome
Oyodo-Ku
Osaka
Japan 531
Tel: (6) 375 1148

Pierre d'Avoine
Architects
Tapestry Court
Mortlake High Street
London SW14
Great Britain
Tel: (081) 878 9455

Ron Brinkers & d'Soto
Engine Room
Spring House
10 Spring Place
London NW5 3BH
Great Britain
Tel: (071) 267 3857

Gianfranco Cavaglia
Architect
via Giolitti N.11
19123 Turin Italy
Tel: (11) 54 81 68

Chassay Architects
90 Westbourne Terrace
London W2
Great Britain
Tel: (071) 402 3233

Chipperfield Associates
1a Cobham Mews
Agar Grove
London NW1 9FB
Great Britain
Tel: (071) 267 9422
Fax: (071) 267 9347

Jo Crepain Architect
De Pretlann 3
Kapellen
2080
Belgium
Tel: (3) 666 4916
Fax: (3) 666 4953

Gary Cunningham
Architects
2700 Fairmount /200
Dallas
Texas 75201
USA
Tel: (214) 855 5272
Fax: (214) 871 3307

Lyman Davies
11 Tomlins Grove
London E4
Great Britain
Tel: (081) 981 4717

Nicholas Grimshaw &
Partners Ltd
1 Conway Street
Fitzroy Square
London W1P 5HA
Tel: (071) 631 0869
Fax: (071) 636 4866

Gwathmey Siegel &
Associates
475 Tenth Avenue
New York
NY 10018
USA
Tel: (212) 947 1240
Fax: (212) 967 0890

Steven Holl Architects
133 West 19th Street
New York
NY 10011
USA
Tel: (212) 989 0918

Arata Isozaki &
Associates
6–14 Akasaka 9 Chome
Minato-Ku
Tokyo
Japan
Tel: (3) 405 1526-9

Eva Jiricna Architects
7 Dering Street
London W1R 9AB
Great Britain
Tel: (071) 629 4541

Peter Leonard
Associates
535 Kings Road
London SW10 0TZ
Great Britain
Tel: (071) 352 1717
Fax: (071) 351 4307

Rick Mather Architects
123 Camden High
Street
London NW1
Great Britain
Tel: (071) 284 1726
Fax: (071) 267 7826

Munkenbeck &
Marshall Architects
113–117 Farringdon
Road
London EC1R
Great Britain
Tel: (071) 833 1407

G Murcutt Associates
176a Raglan Street
Mosman
NSW 2088
Australia
Tel: (2) 969 7797

Brian Murphy
B.A.M. Construction/
Design Inc
1422 Second Street
Santa Monica
CA 90401
USA
Tel: (213) 393 3252
Fax: (213) 393 3812

John Pawson
77 New Bond Street
London W1Y 9DB
Great Britain
Tel: (071) 495 1212

Richard Rogers &
Partners
Rianville Road
Thames Wharf
London W6 9HA
Great Britain
Tel: (071) 385 1235
Fax: (071) 385 8409

Birds Portchmouth
Russum Architects
Shoreditch Studio
44–46 Scrutton Street
London EC2A 4HH
Great Britain
Tel: (071) 377 2777
Fax: (071) 377 5439

Shinohara Atelier
1622 Tao-Cho
Kohoku-Ku
Yokohama 7222
Japan
Tel: (45) 541 0099

Claudio Silvestrin
Architect
35 Alfred Place
London WC1
Great Britain
Tel: (071) 323 6545

Tsao McKown Architects
Suite 1610
41 East 42nd Street
New York
NY 10017
USA
Tel: (212) 697 0980

Andreas Weber
Nymphenburgerstrasse
79
8000 München 19
Germany
Tel: (89) 123 4551

David Wild Design &
Build
44 Rochester Place
London NW1
Great Britain
Tel: (071) 267 7126

Peter Wilson
Studio 3
5 Thurloe Square
London SW7
Great Britain
Tel: (071) 589 7560

INDEX

Richard Bryant and Arcaid would like to thank all the home owners for their hospitality during the often disruptive process of photography.

Further appreciation goes to our friends at Ambiente for their continuous support in finding locations.